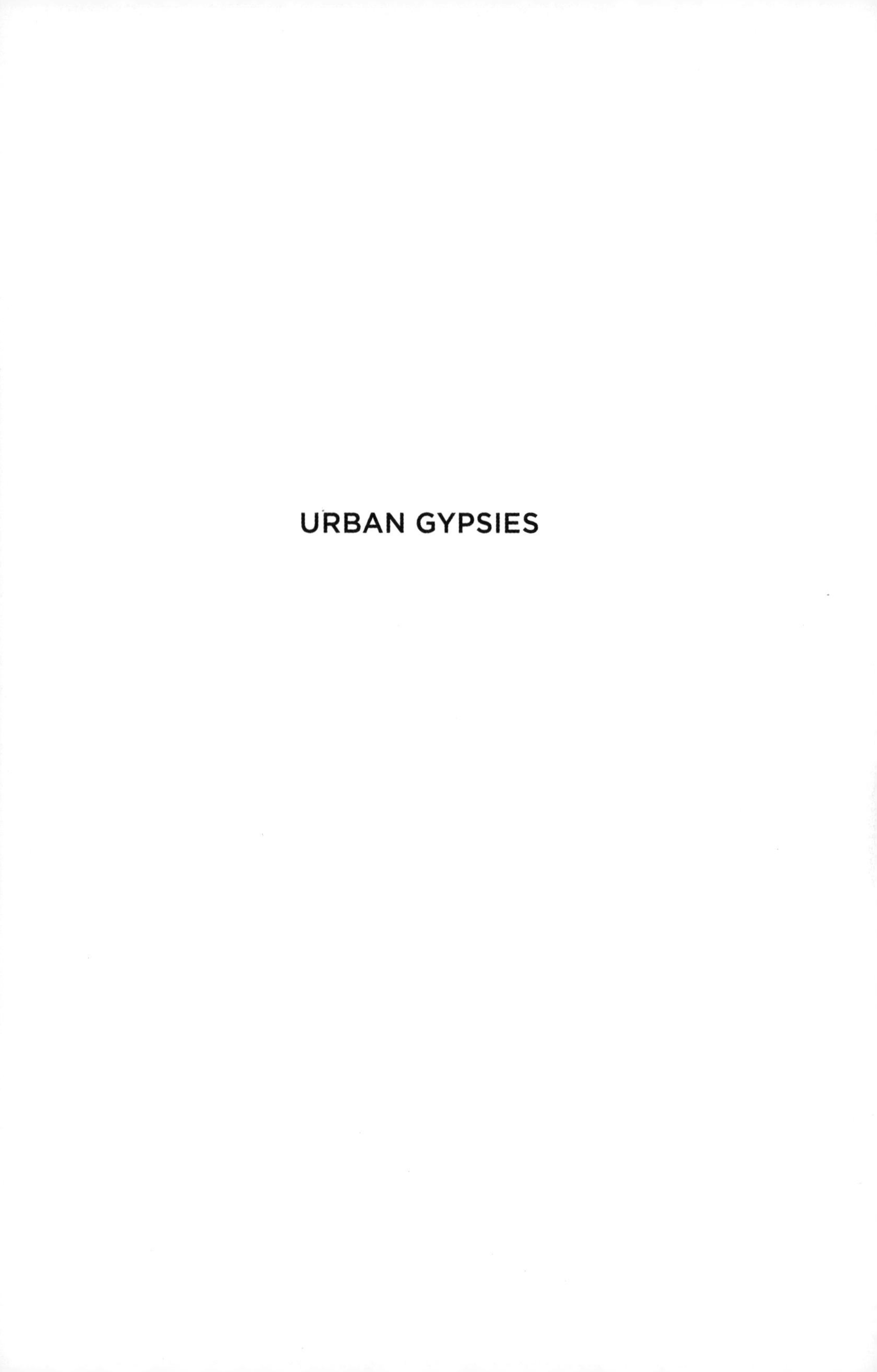

URBAN GYPSIES

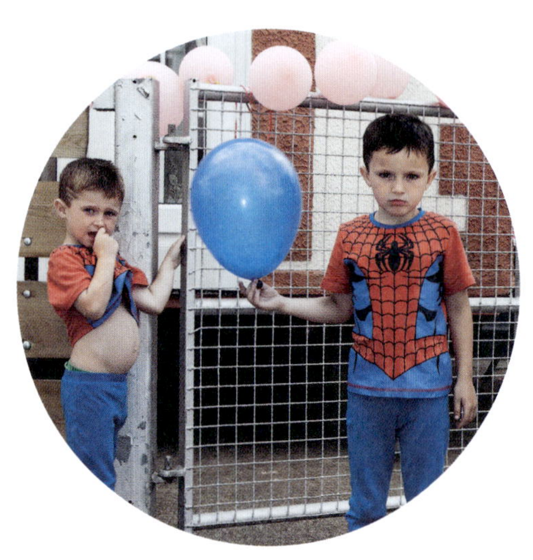

URBAN GYPSIES

PAUL WENHAM-CLARKE

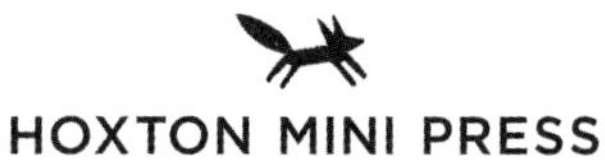

HOXTON MINI PRESS

Also in the series

Book One
People of London

Book Two
On the Night Bus

Book Three
London Youth

Book Four
Urban Dirt Bikers

Book Five
New York Waterways

Book Six
Botanical

Book Seven
Berlin Nights

Book Eight
London's Square Mile

This book is available as a collector's edition

www.hoxtonminipress.com

From the series

TALES FROM THE CITY

Book Nine

INTRODUCTION

by Rachel Segal Hamilton

The Westway curls from Paddington to North Kensington, a colossal grey serpent, choking West London in its grip. Like so many constructions of the 1960s and 70s, it can look irredeemably ugly to contemporary eyes but its conception was utopian. This 3.5 miles of continuous concrete was built between 1964 and 1970 to alleviate congestion, an elevated, eight-lane dual carriageway leading commuters in and out of the capital, from the office in town to suburban bliss on the outskirts. As with all developments, the project had its losers: some residents' homes were cleared to make way for the new road. But one group remained.

Stable Way, near Latimer Road in the borough of Kensington and Chelsea, has been a 'stopping place' for Travellers since the 19th century. Officially designated as a Traveller's site in 1976, it's now home to some 20 Irish Traveller families. Early in the morning, as he drove along the A4 into London to work as an advertising photographer, Paul Wenham-Clarke would catch a glimpse of their static caravans and trailers, along with mechanics' workshops, football pitches, stables, a school – a whole world thriving in this inauspicious setting.

In 2011 he set out to document the entire length of the Westway, but remained most intrigued by Stable Way. Paul is Professor of Photography at Arts University Bournemouth and his university gave him time and funding to undertake this project. Wary of aggravation, he adopted a roundabout approach, initially photographing everyone except the Travellers. Each time, he'd casually mention his interest in photographing the Travellers. Eventually it paid off. Eight months into the two-year project, he received a call from Pat, a well respected long-term resident of the Westway Traveller site. They agreed Wenham-Clarke could photograph the Travellers, but only on their terms, covering family events or celebrations, always asking permission as he went.

As a result, many of the shots show the Travellers at formal occasions, christenings, anniversaries or birthday parties. This isn't documentary photography in the candid tradition – it's clear in the hands on sparkly hips or heads tilted towards the camera that they're conscious of the camera and Wenham-Clarke's use of lighting give the shots a sleeker feel. But this makes it no less authentic, perhaps more in a way. After all, we now know that idea of the photographer as an impartial observer who hits the shutter and captures 'what's there' to be a myth. A photograph is the end result of many choices, from framing to editing. Through this close collaboration the Travellers are deciding how they want to be represented.

And who can blame them for wanting to take control of their own image? Travellers, also known as Gypsies, are a subject of fascination to wider society, endlessly misrepresented, exoticised or mocked, from Bizet's sexy, dangerous Carmen to Brad Pitt's comic turn as an incomprehensible bare-knuckle boxer in *Snatch*. The best-known recent depiction is the TV series *My Big Fat Gypsy Wedding*, which invited us to gawp and sneer in 'a narrative that's part *Stars in Their Eyes*, part nature show', as the author and former *Travellers' Times* editor Damian Le Bas puts it.

Over the past decades, British Travellers have seen their right to culturally appropriate housing eroded. The 1994 Criminal Justice Act took away special protections for Travellers' sites and the 2016 Housing and Planning Act did away with protections for those with a 'cultural tradition of nomadism or of living in a caravan'. Today, the 17,000 Travellers estimated to be living in London are facing a housing crisis. As property developers circle, the Travellers of the Westway fear their time here is limited. And moving on most likely means moving away from each other.

There's poignancy in shots in which the huge road looms above, or a young boy sits in a broken toy car. No longer able to live the nomadic life, the Travellers find shelter in the shade of society's more sanctioned form of travel. But this interpretation doesn't tell the whole story. It's a common mistake among outsiders to think that Travellers are only Travellers if they're on the go. London is their home. What Wenham-Clarke's pictures show is that Traveller life is fundamentally about community. On site, inside and outside blur, caravan doors swing open, kids play and leap, not a screen in sight. Freedom isn't just the freedom to escape – it's also the freedom to be together.

This is the story of my photography road trip, not along the road, but under it.

Beneath the Westway, an elevated highway in West London, lives a group of Irish Travellers. I used to pass over their heads on my way to photographic studios to the east of the city and would often wonder about their lives and their story.

Who lived there and why?

I decided to pay a visit.

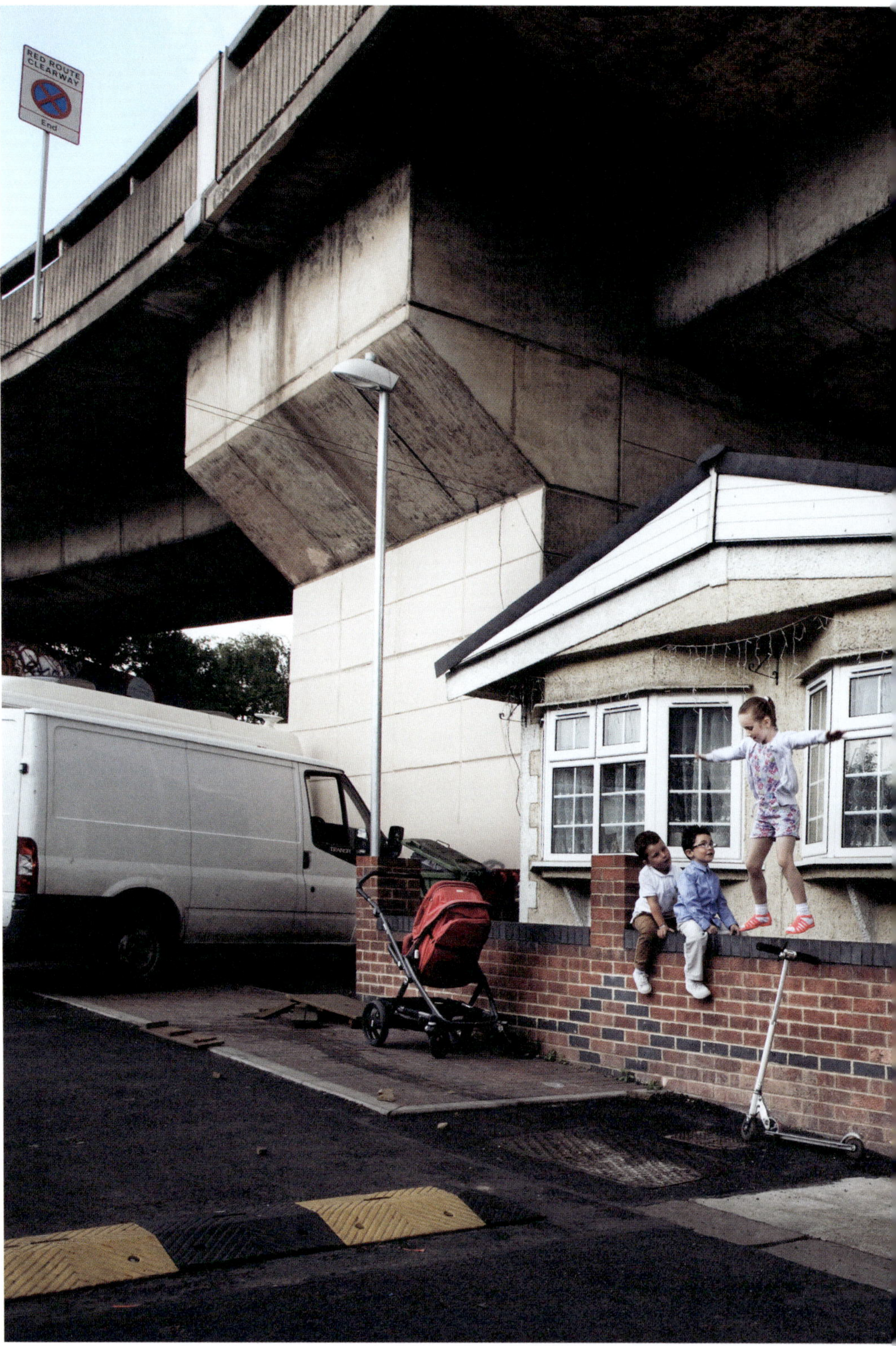

RED ROUTE
CLEARWAY
End

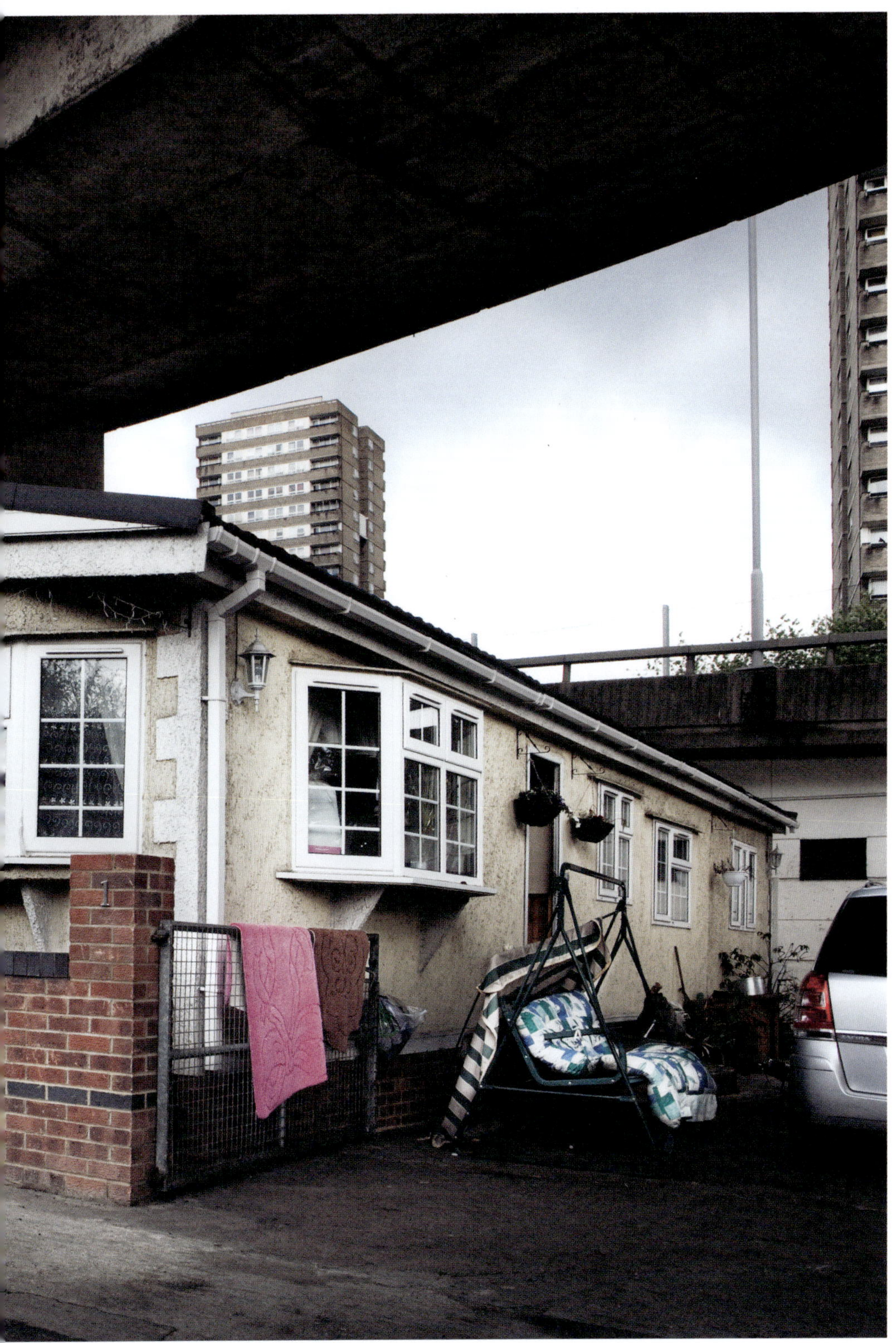

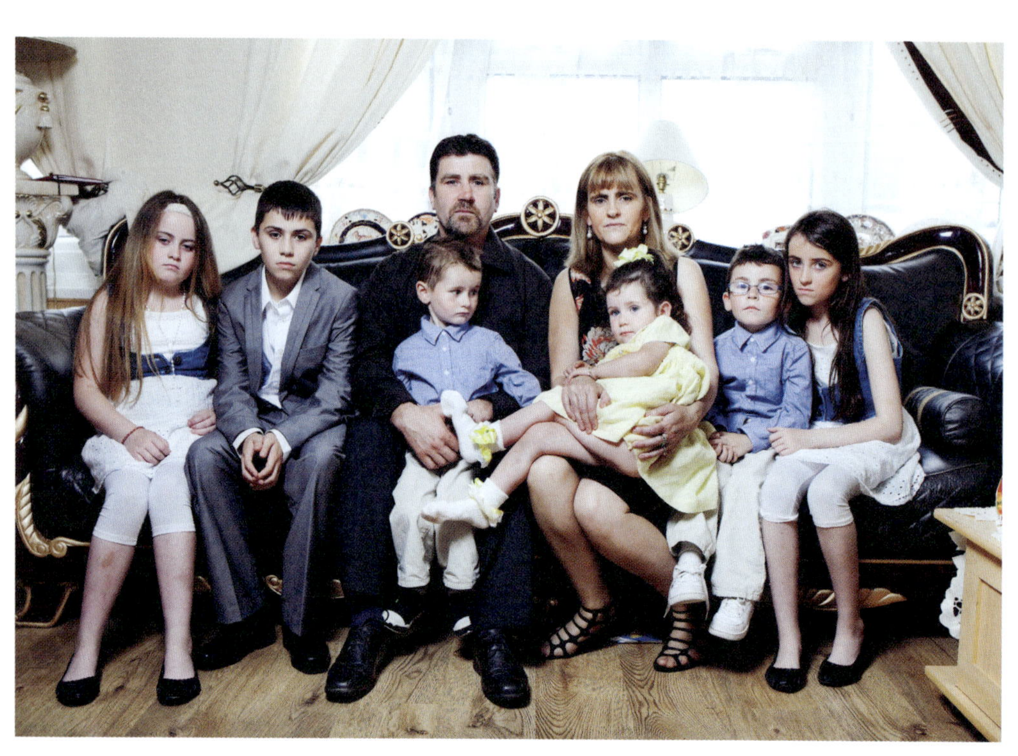

Pat O'Donnell is a long-standing resident of the Westway Traveller site who generously invited me into his home. With his approval I would become accepted by this fascinating group.

The children have an old-fashioned kind of childhood. They play outside for hours a day, running around in groups, using skipping ropes and squirting water.

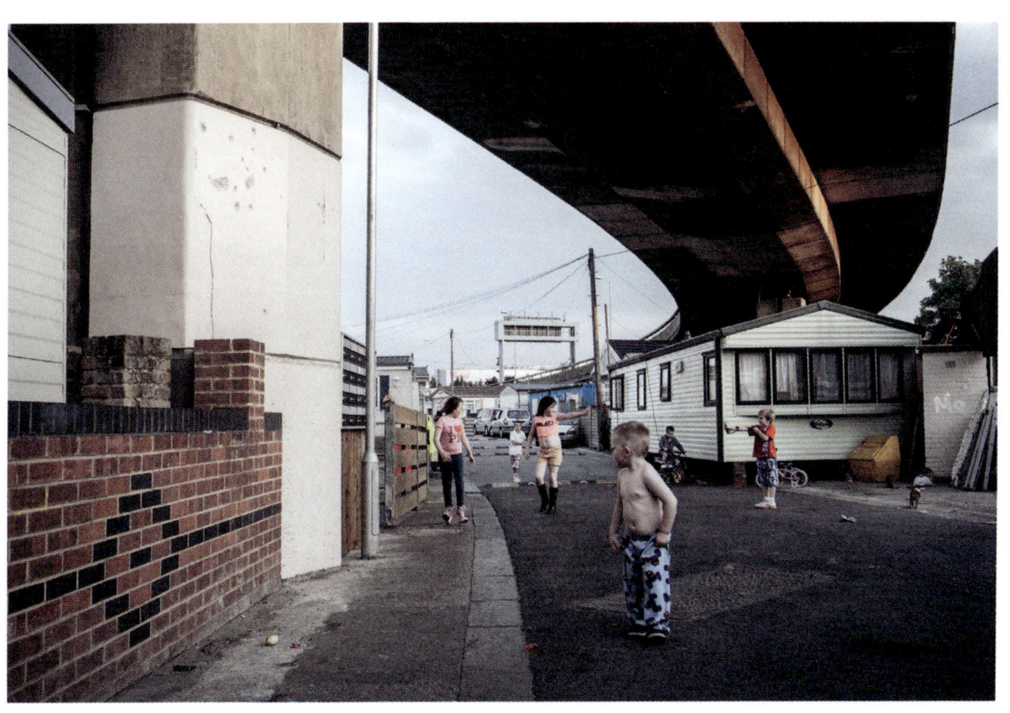

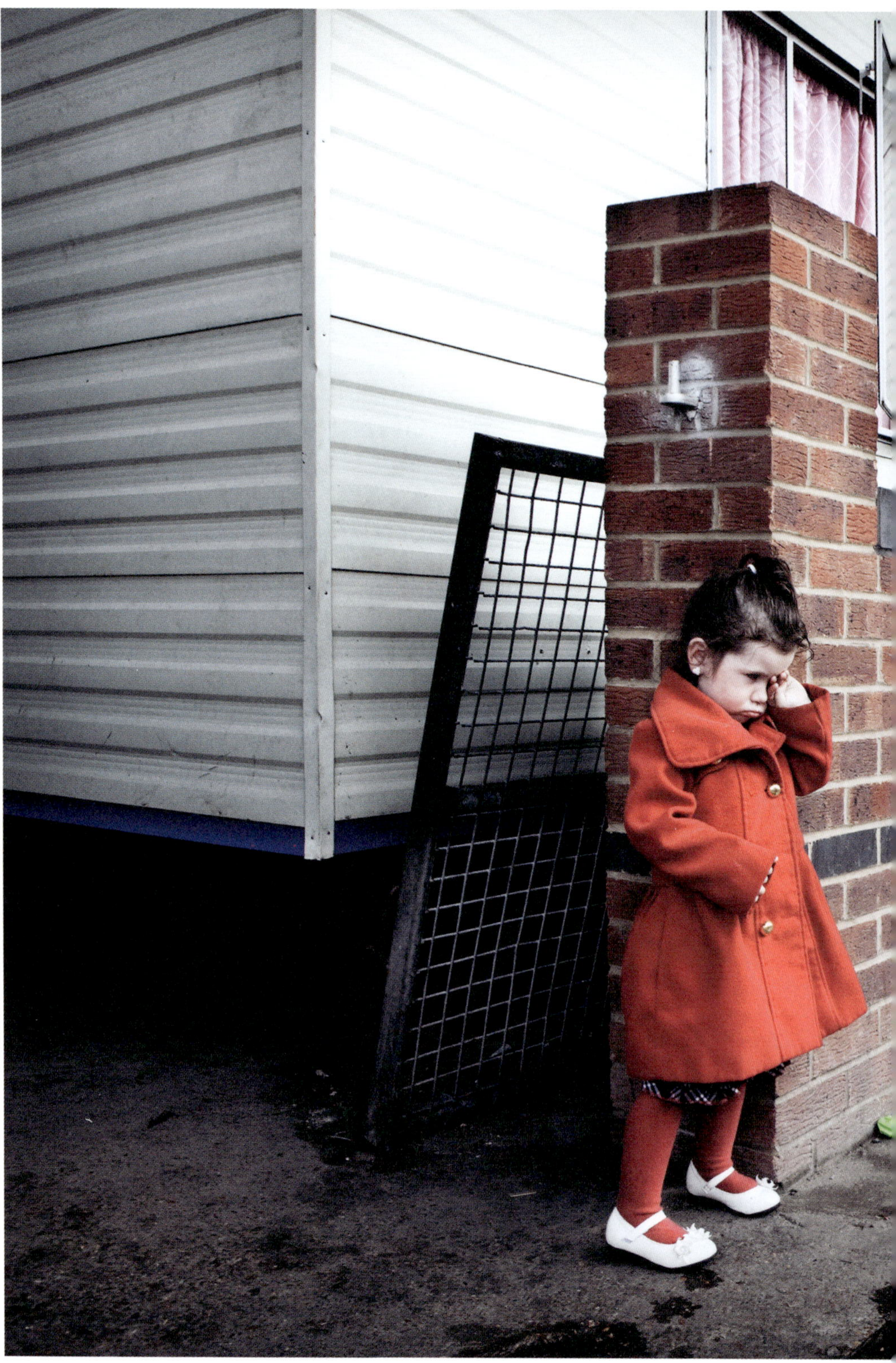

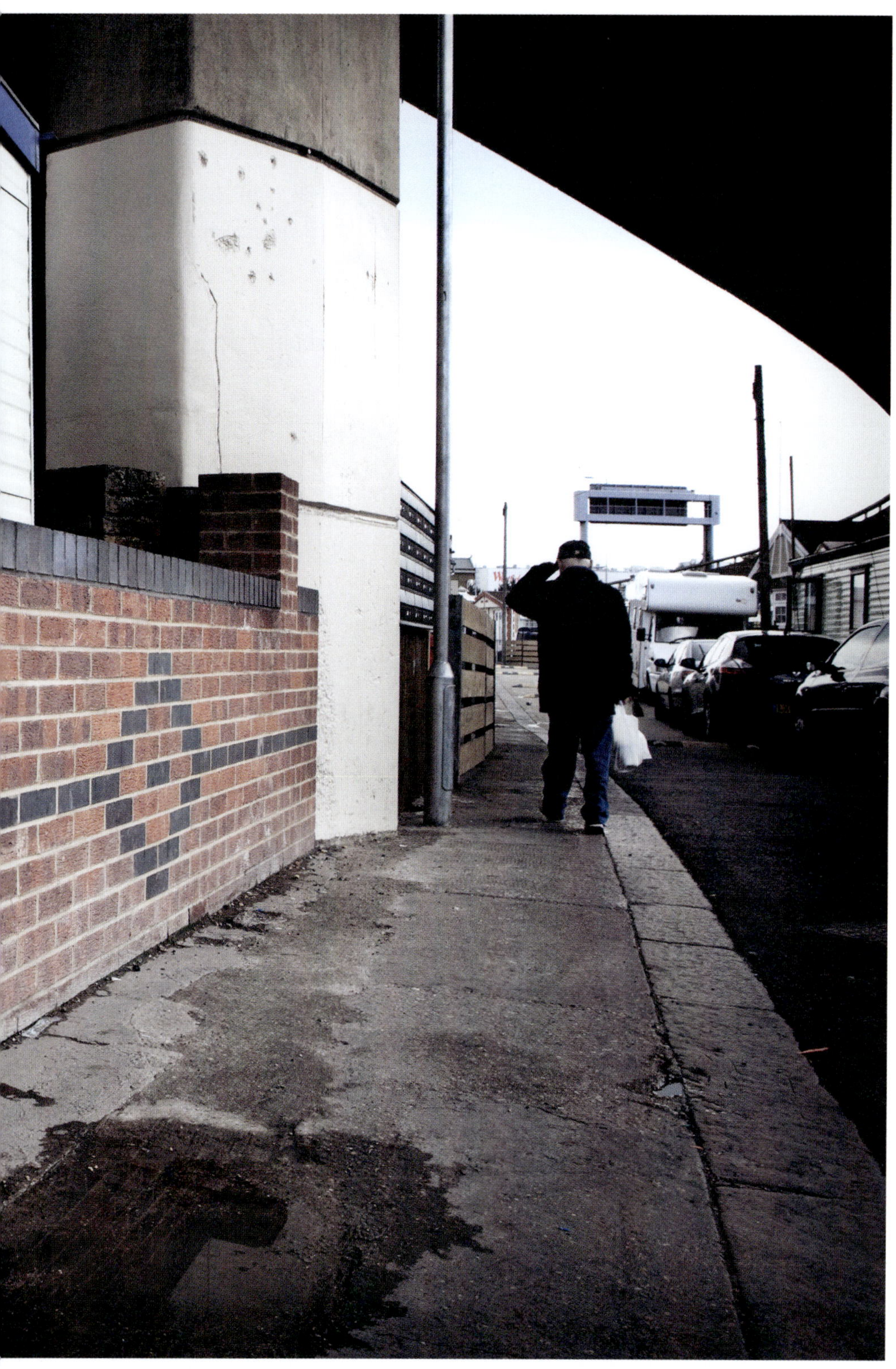

Older kids watch over the youngsters and the children roam around going in and out of different families' caravans, treating each as if it were their own home.

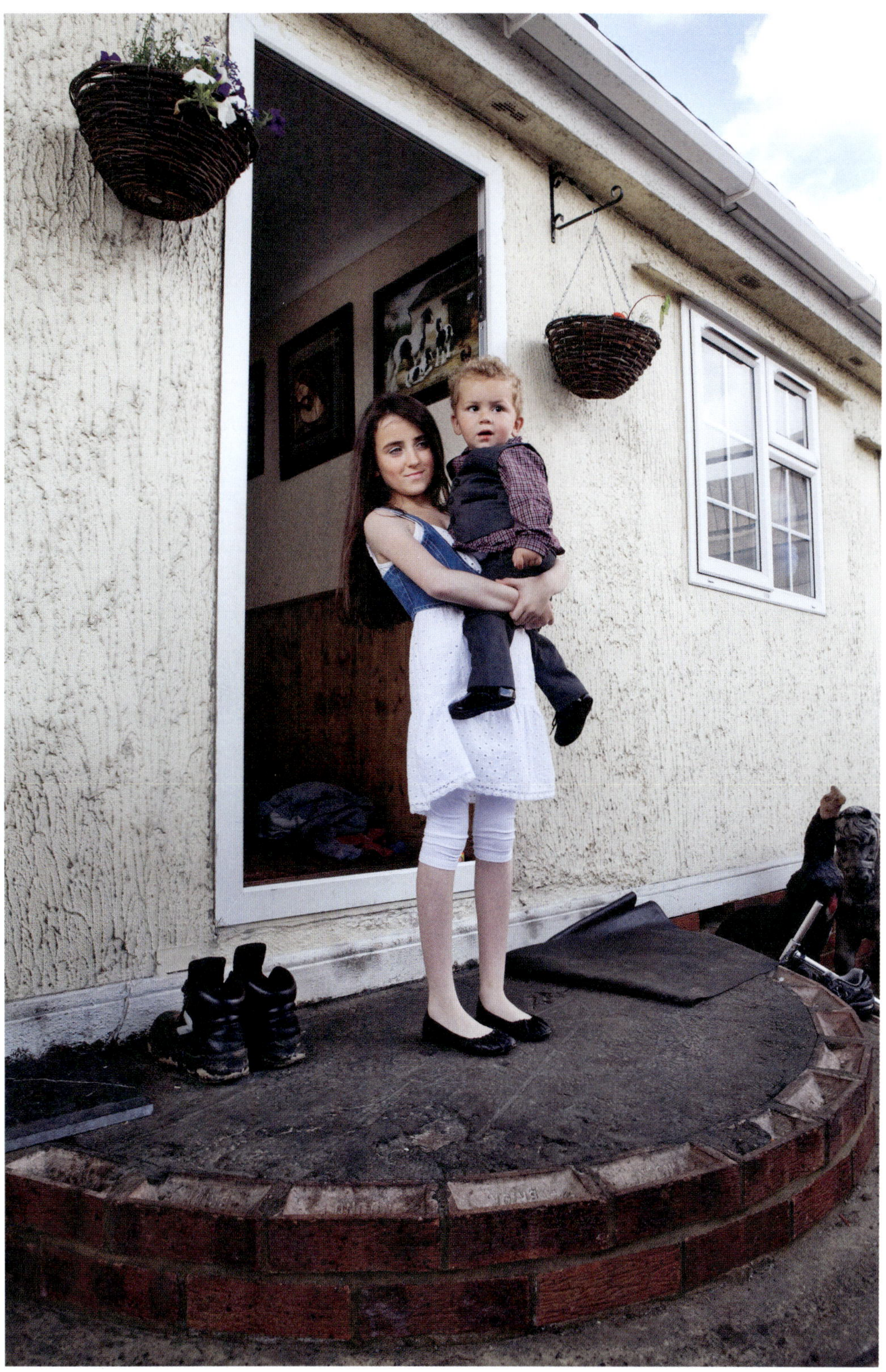

This is an Irish Traveller community and so predominately Catholic. Many of the families regularly go to church on Sunday. They get dressed up in their best, including the kids.

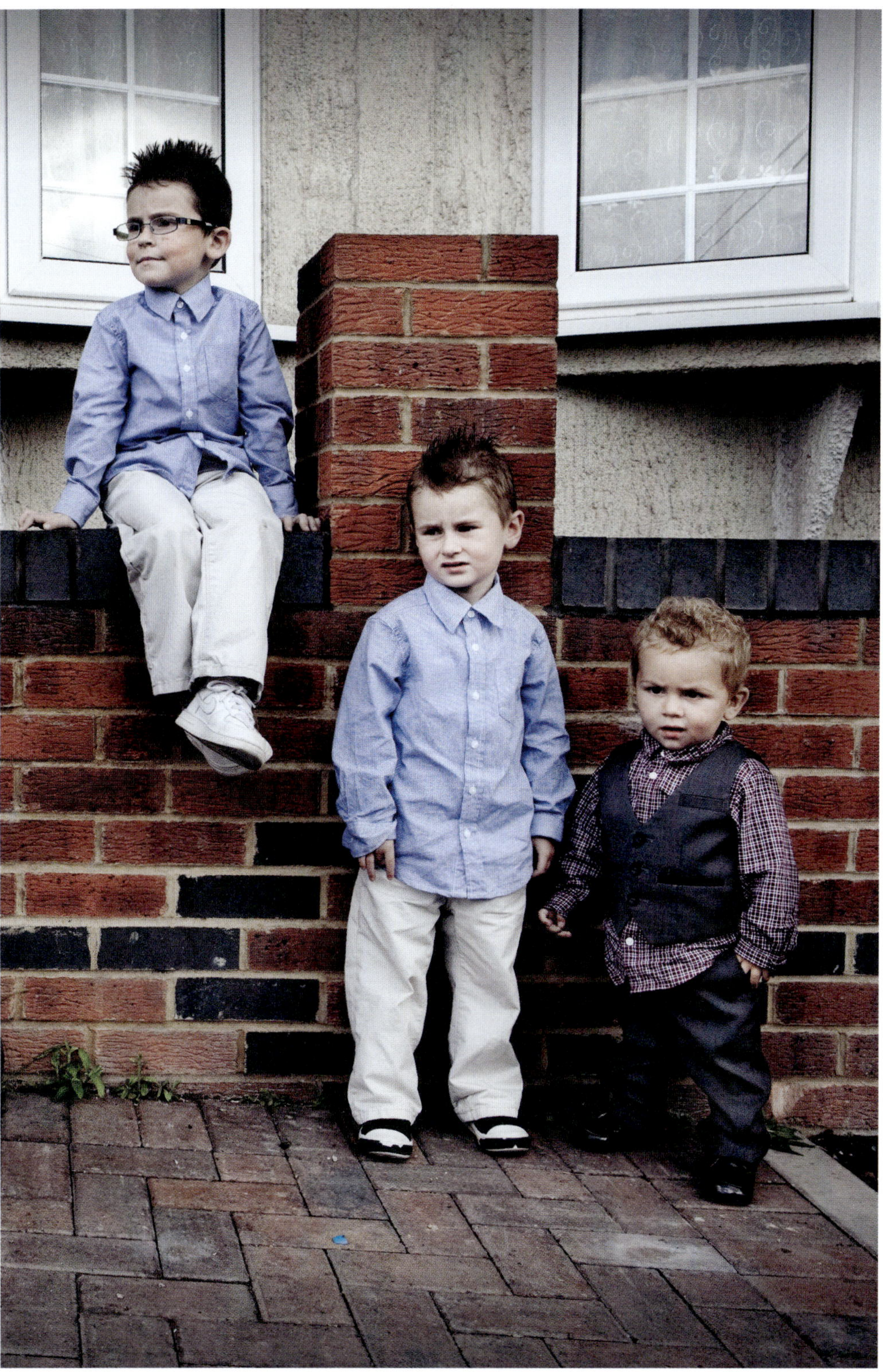

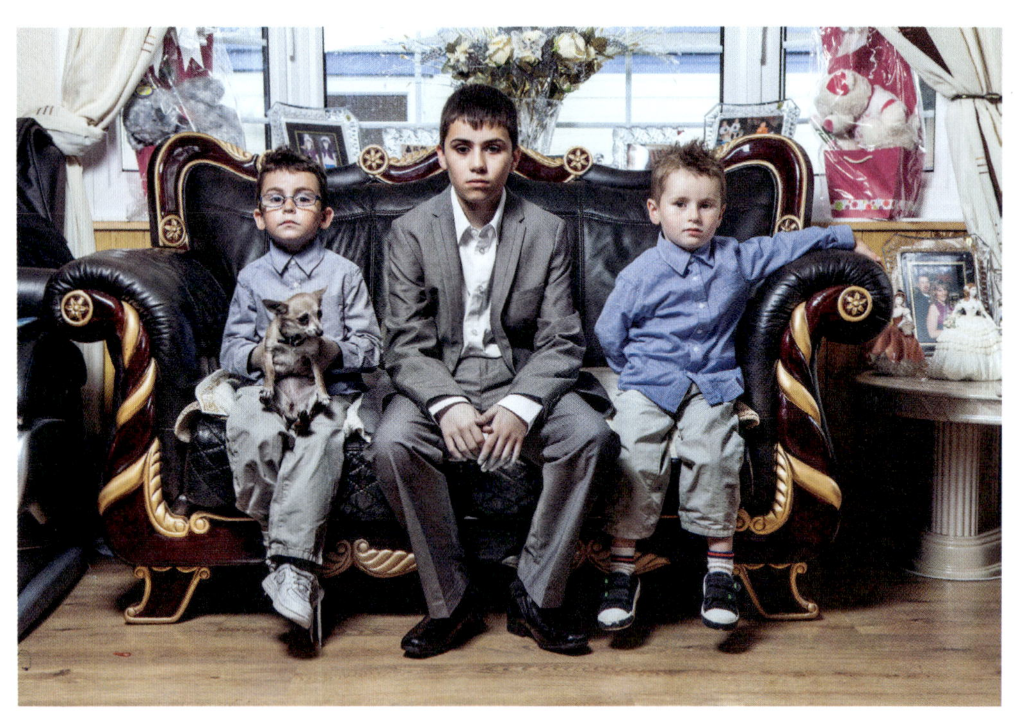

Pat and I came to an agreement that I would photograph all kinds of social events for the community including first communions, birthday parties, weddings and wedding anniversaries. In return I would be able to use the images in my exhibition and this book.

It was a wonderful way to work; all the community got to know me.

Most of the men did not want to be photographed; they were afraid they would lose work if they were identified as Travellers by outsiders. They had many experiences of people cancelling work and not saying why. I agreed not to take fly-on-the-wall images of the adults and this meant I had to take a more formal, posed portrait approach which runs through most of the work.

This is John O'Donnell, former Commonwealth Welterweight Champion, just before he went to Las Vegas for a big fight.

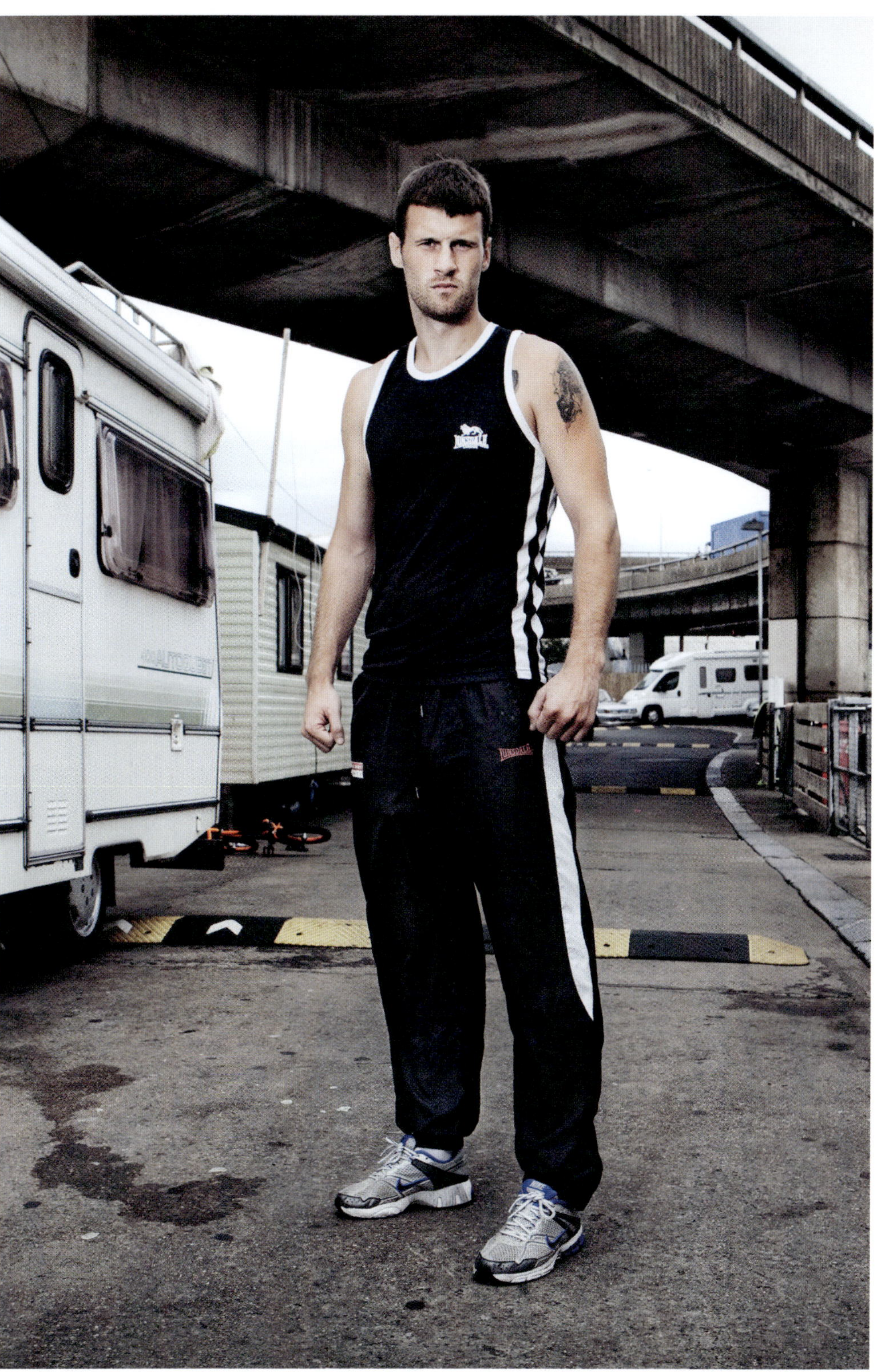

Here are Pat's daughters, Cindy and Shirley, holding their cousin Terry on his Christening Day. The girls were very proud when this picture was displayed in the National Portrait Gallery a year later.

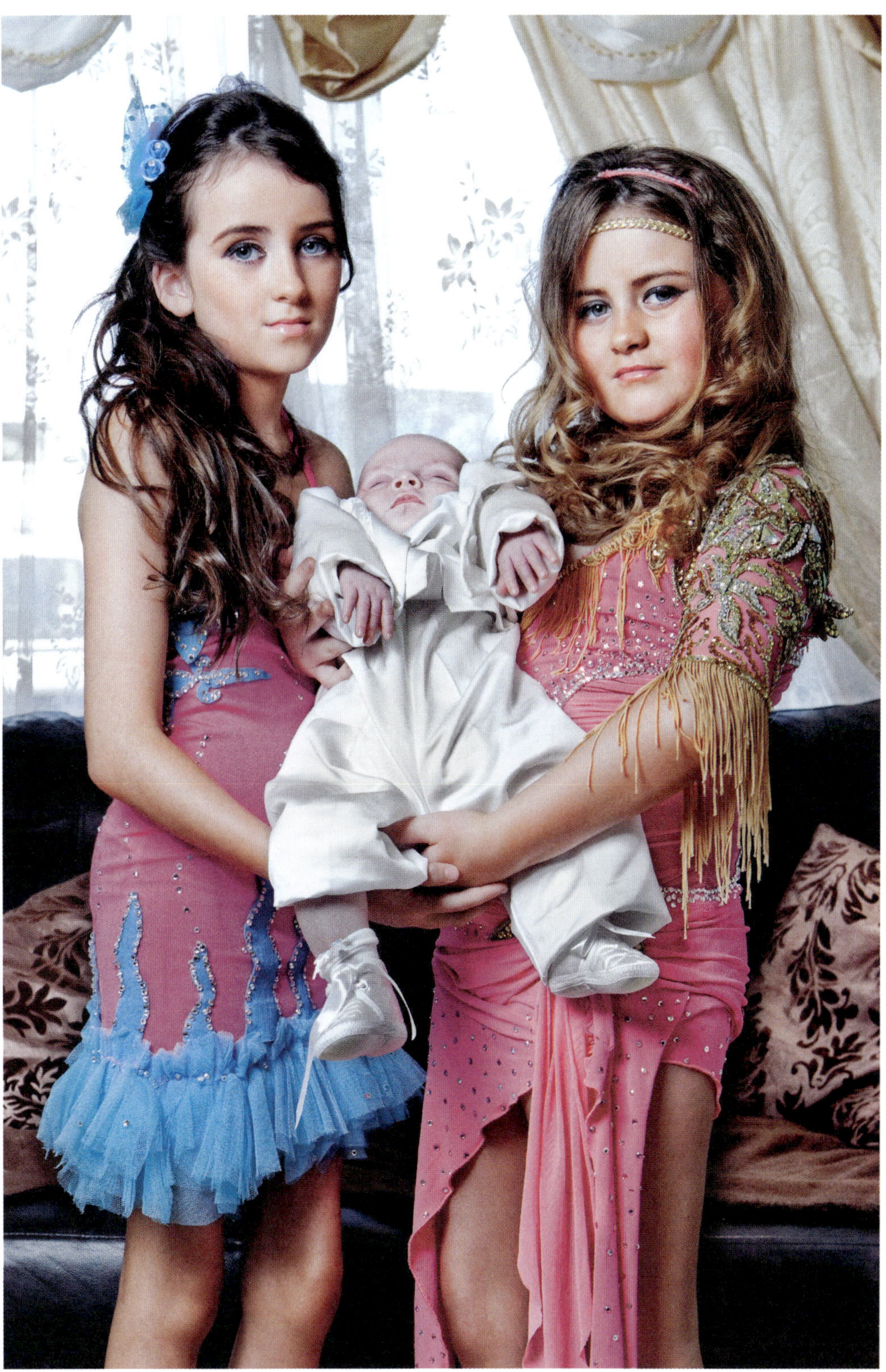

It was a great day – I was made very welcome. I set up my gear in Terry's mother's home and all the relatives took turns to hold him.

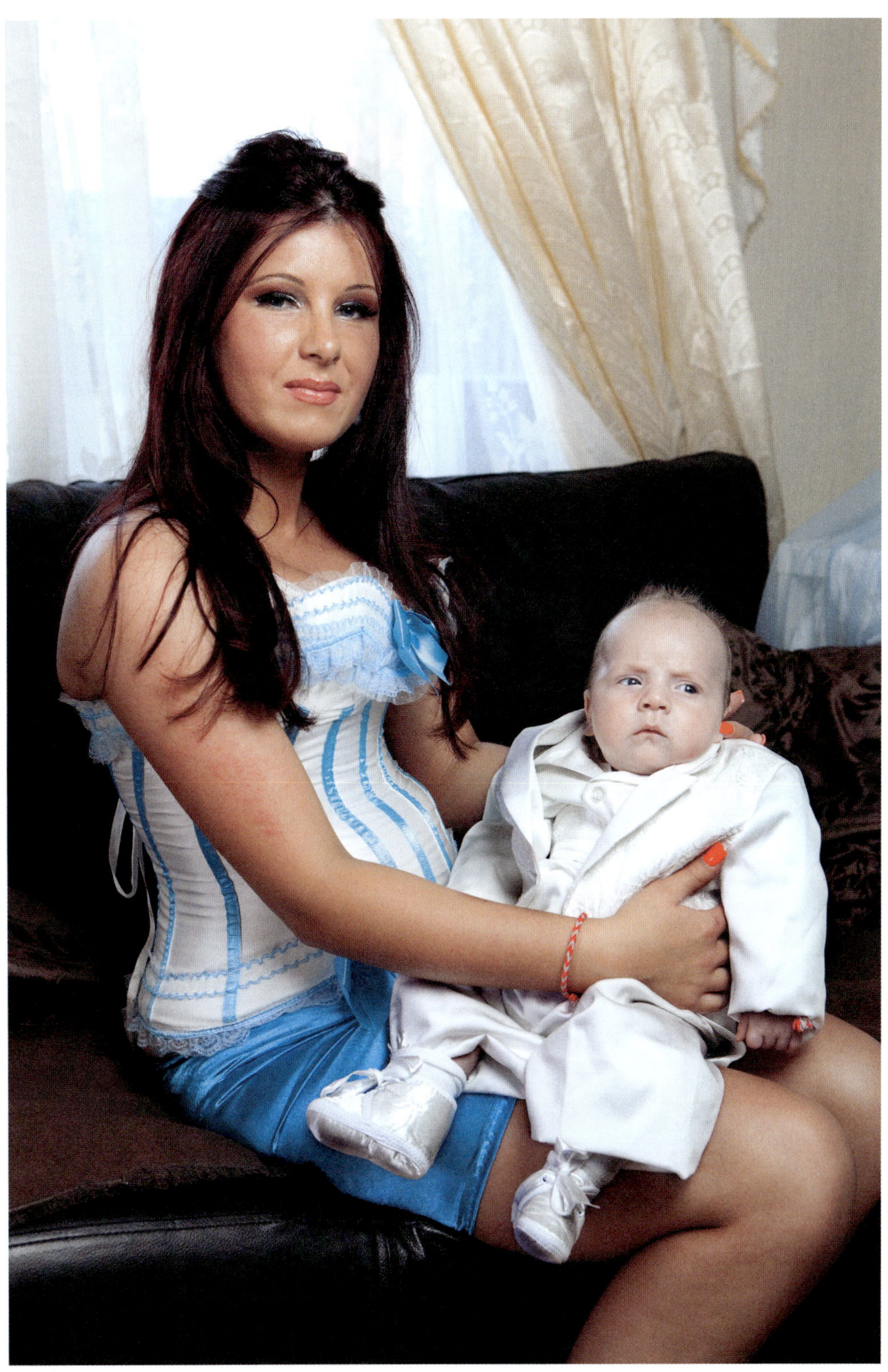

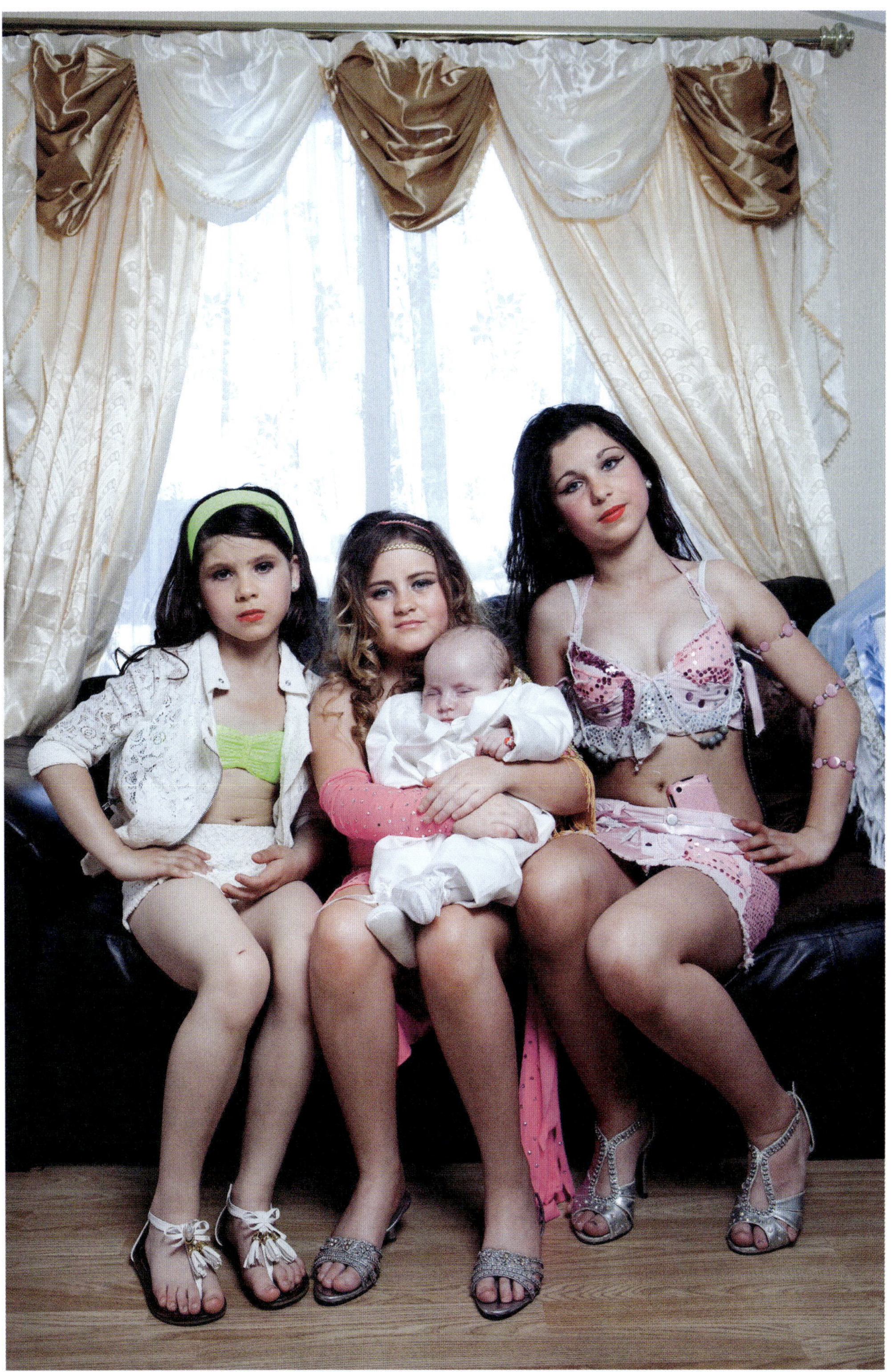

I asked some of the Travellers what they thought of us non-Travellers. They said we were obsessed about owning everything and longed for retirement and didn't live our lives for today.

They couldn't understand why we didn't live with our extended families in close knit communities like they do.

They call themselves 'Gypsies' or 'Travellers', but we are known as 'Gorgers' which means a non-traveller person.

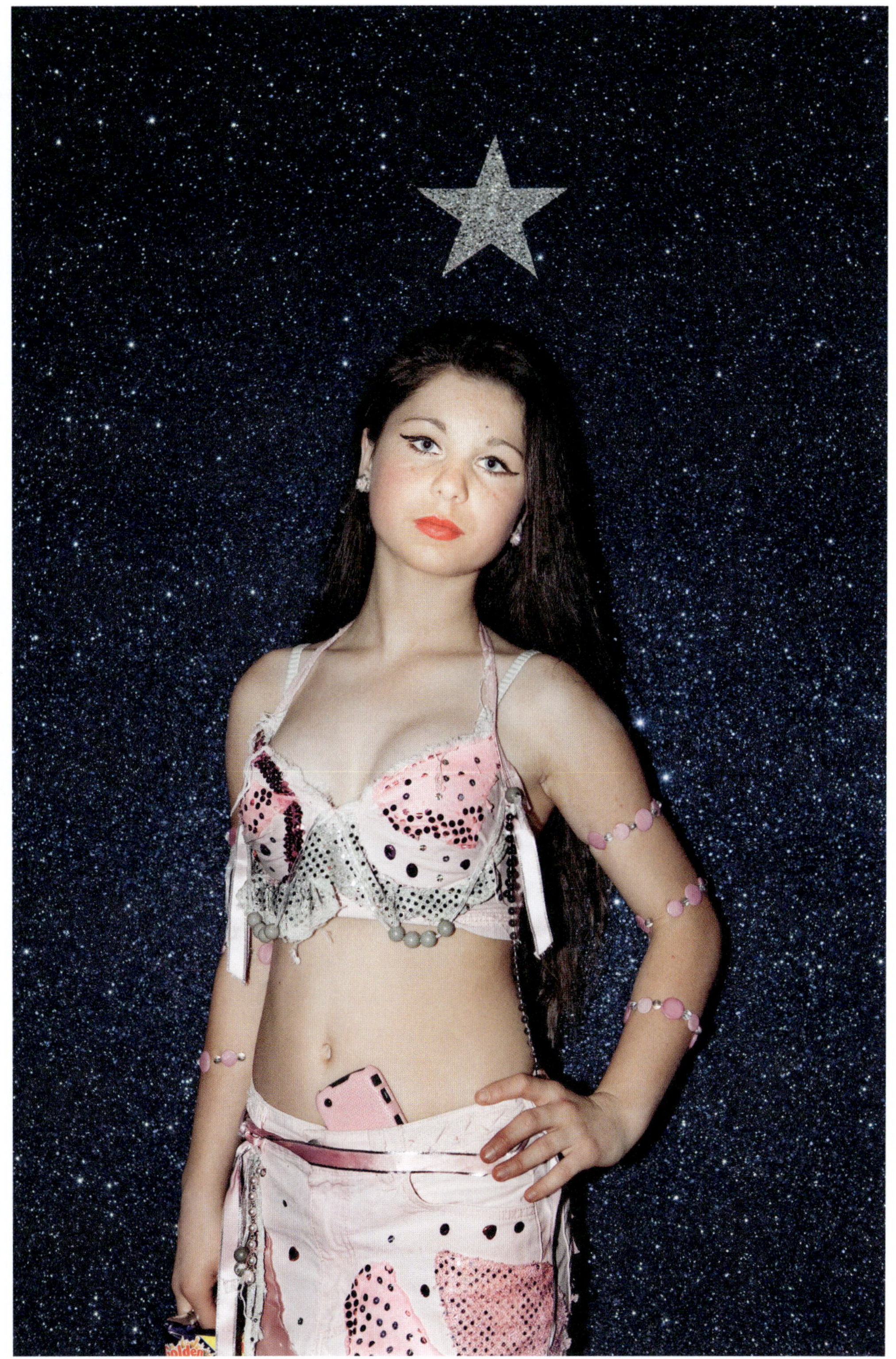

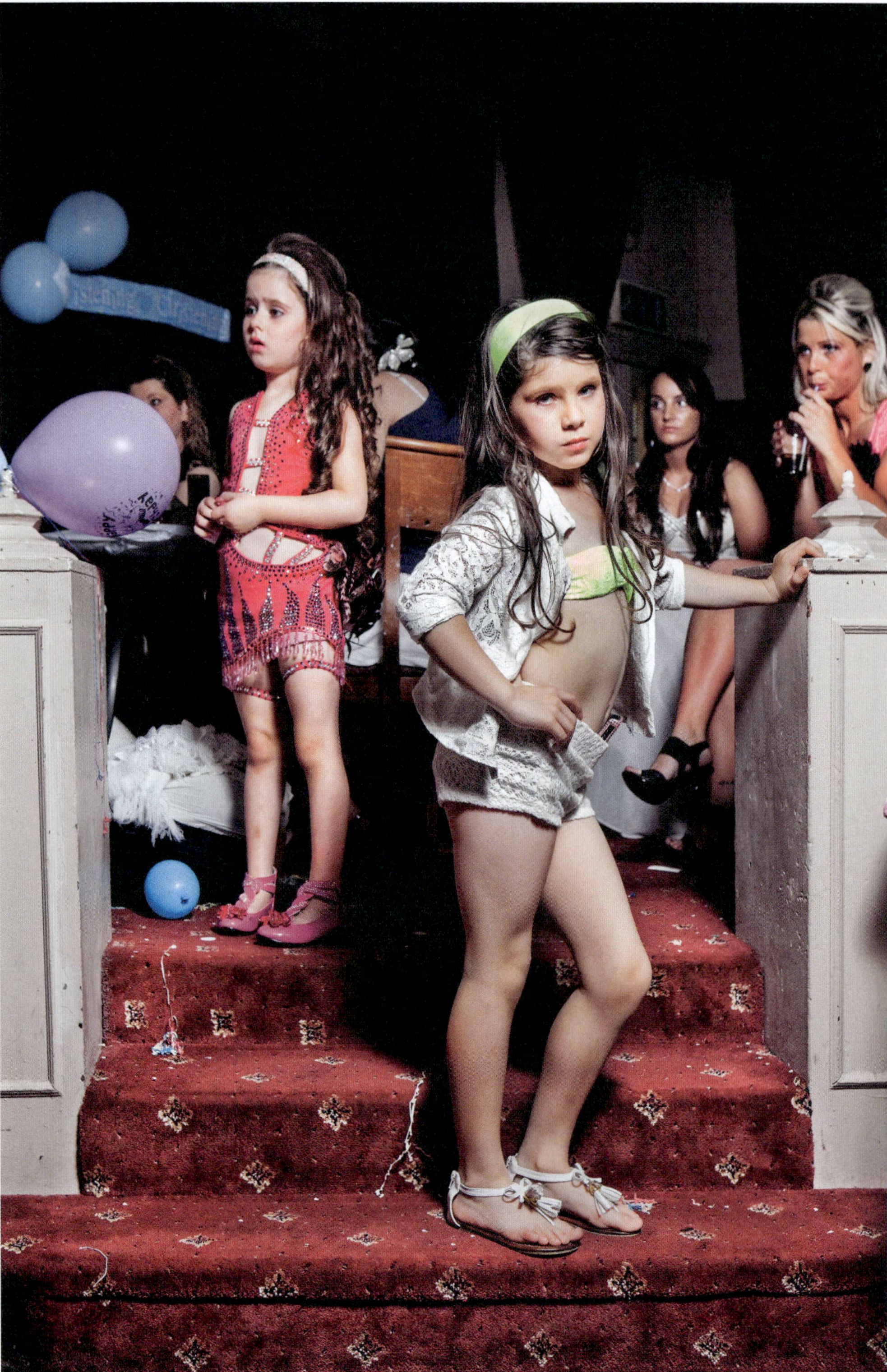

The children had their own tiny makeshift school on the site, but after a few years the families wanted to send them to the local school and so the Traveller school closed.

The head teacher was very welcoming and now all the kids attend the local school. Some have even gone on to college.

As a result, many of the younger Travellers have met partners outside their community and this new generation have lost their will to roam. The parents wanted their children to get a proper education but didn't realise that this would lead to the gradual demise of their culture.

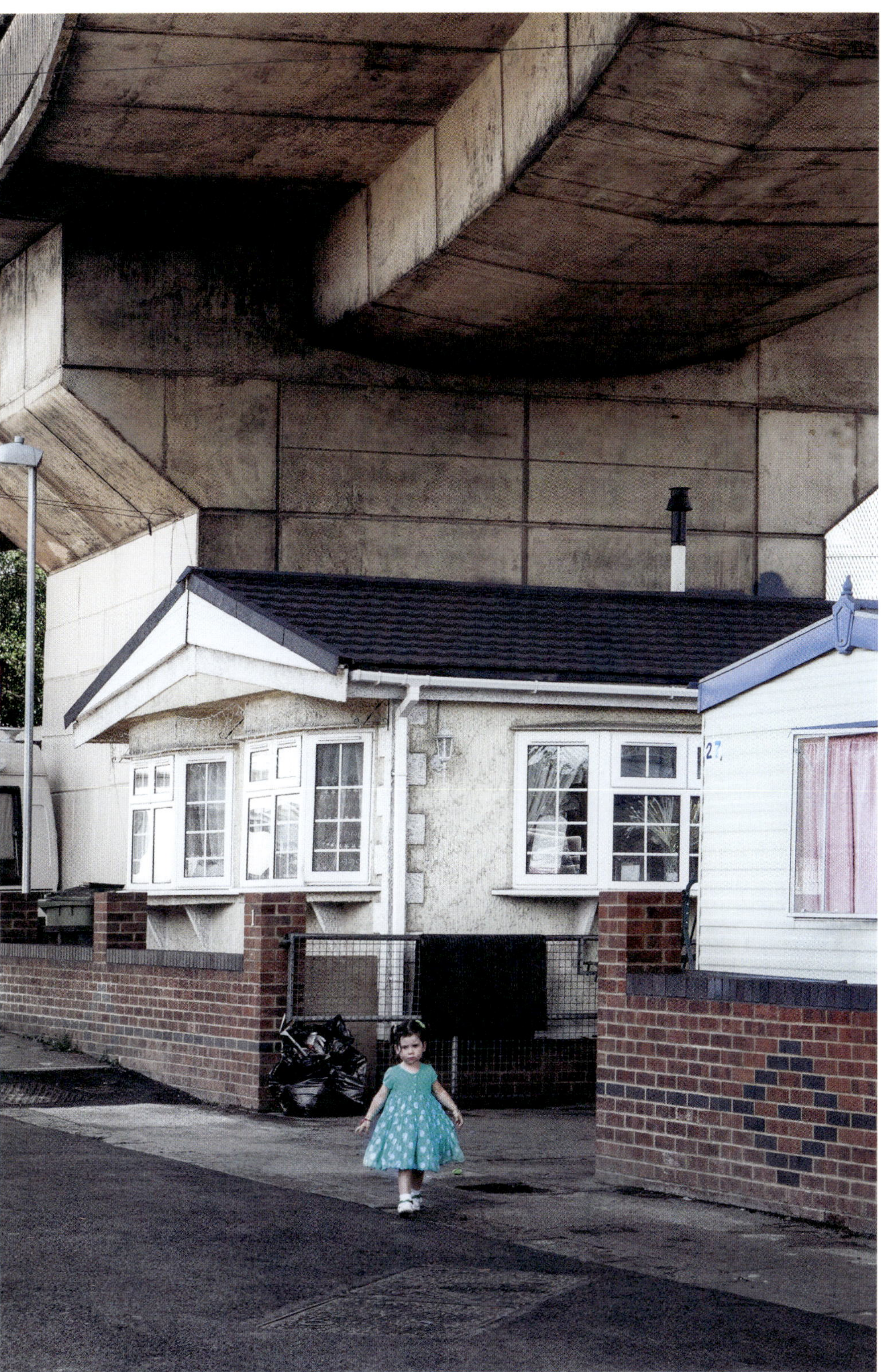

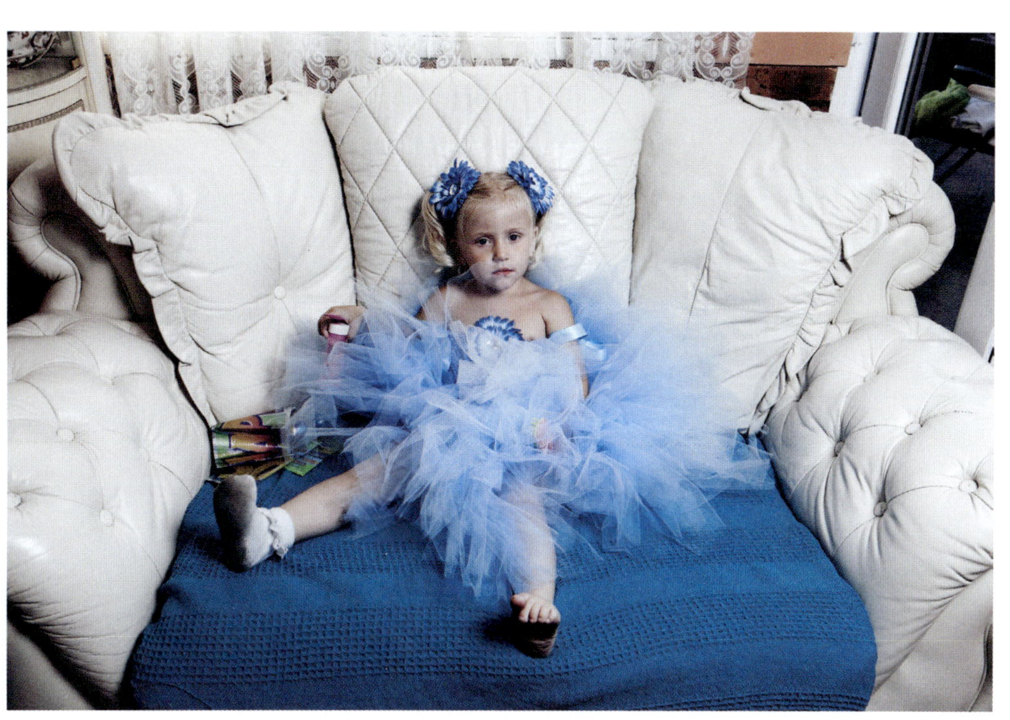

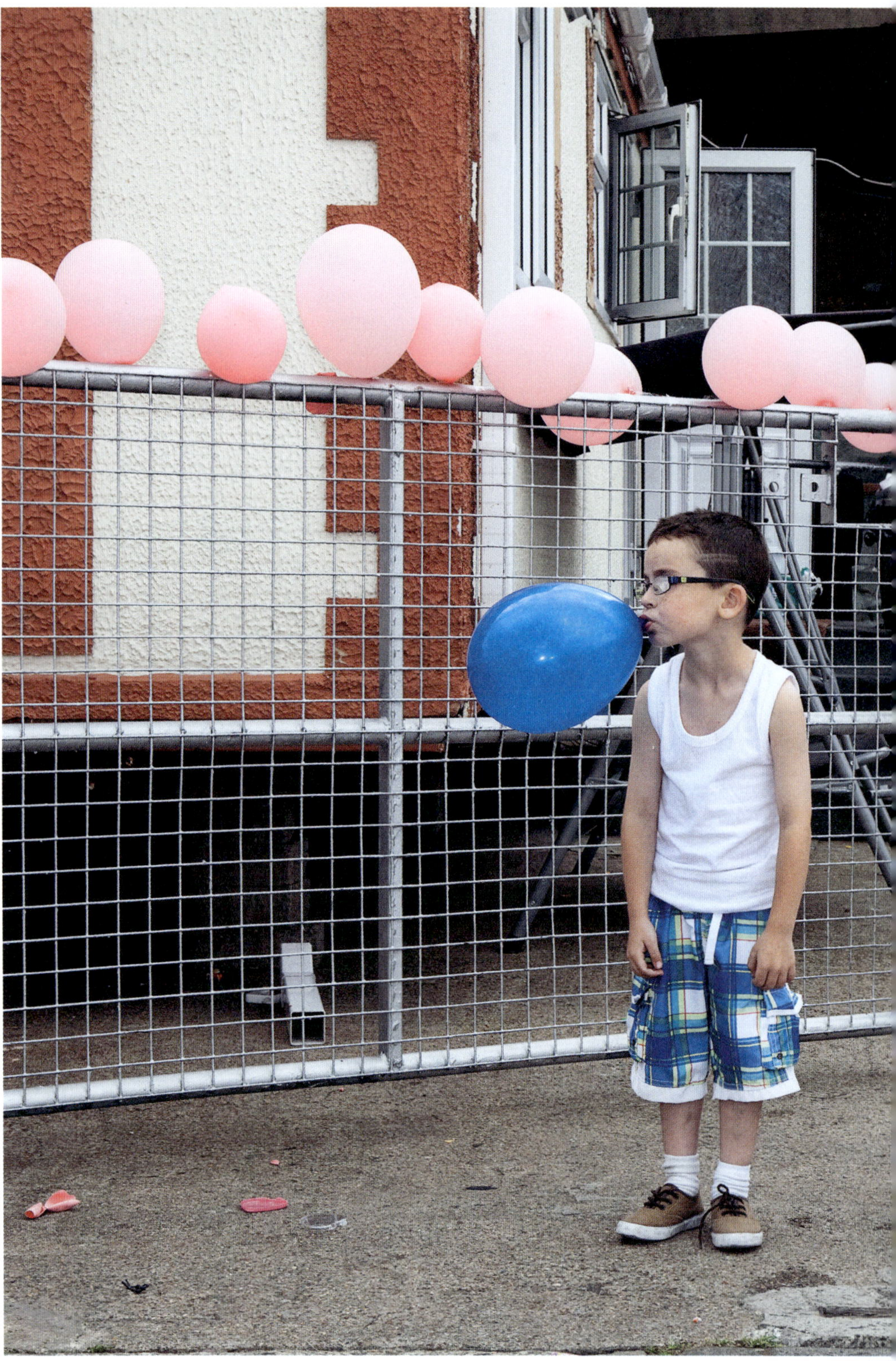

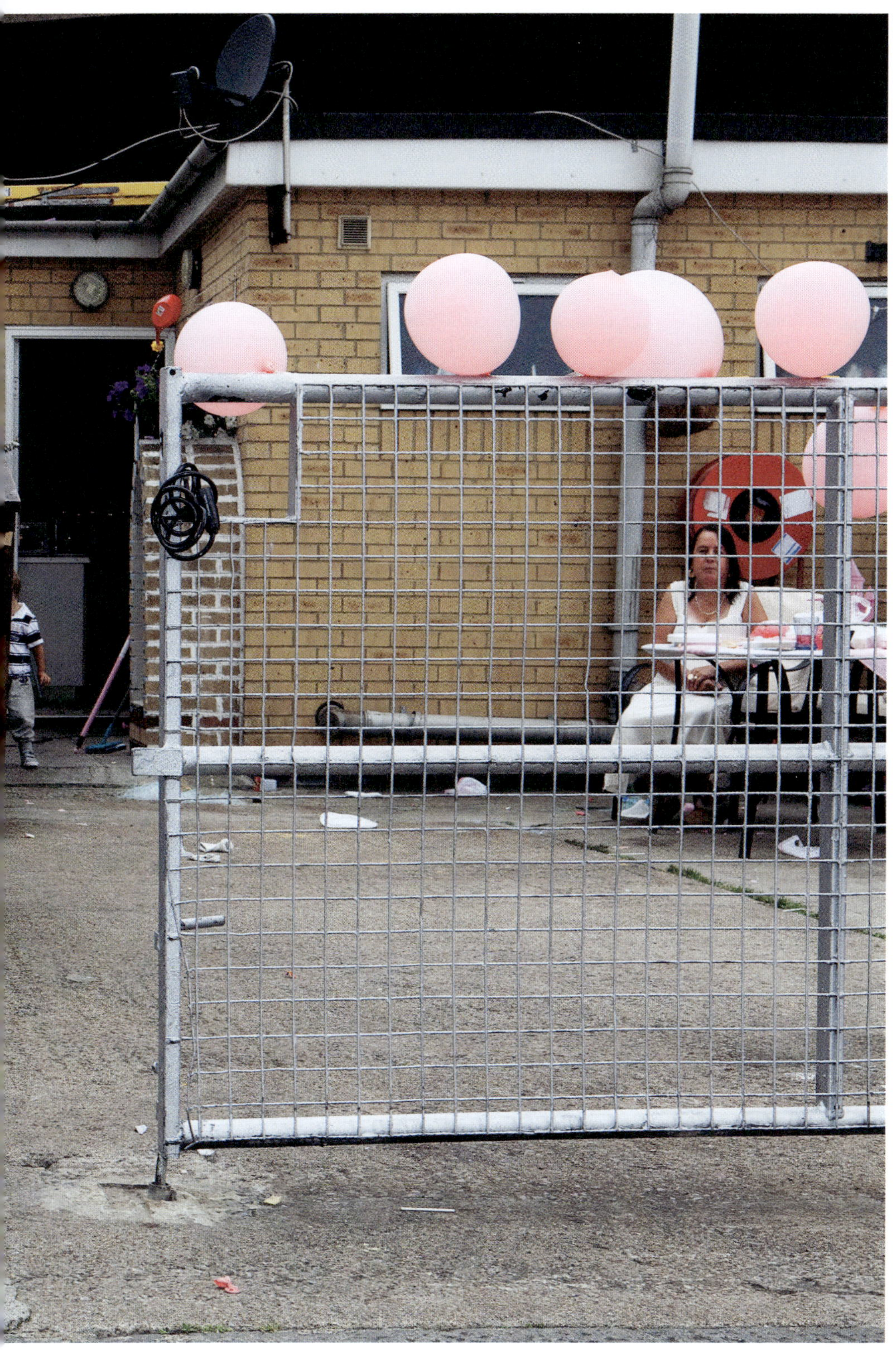

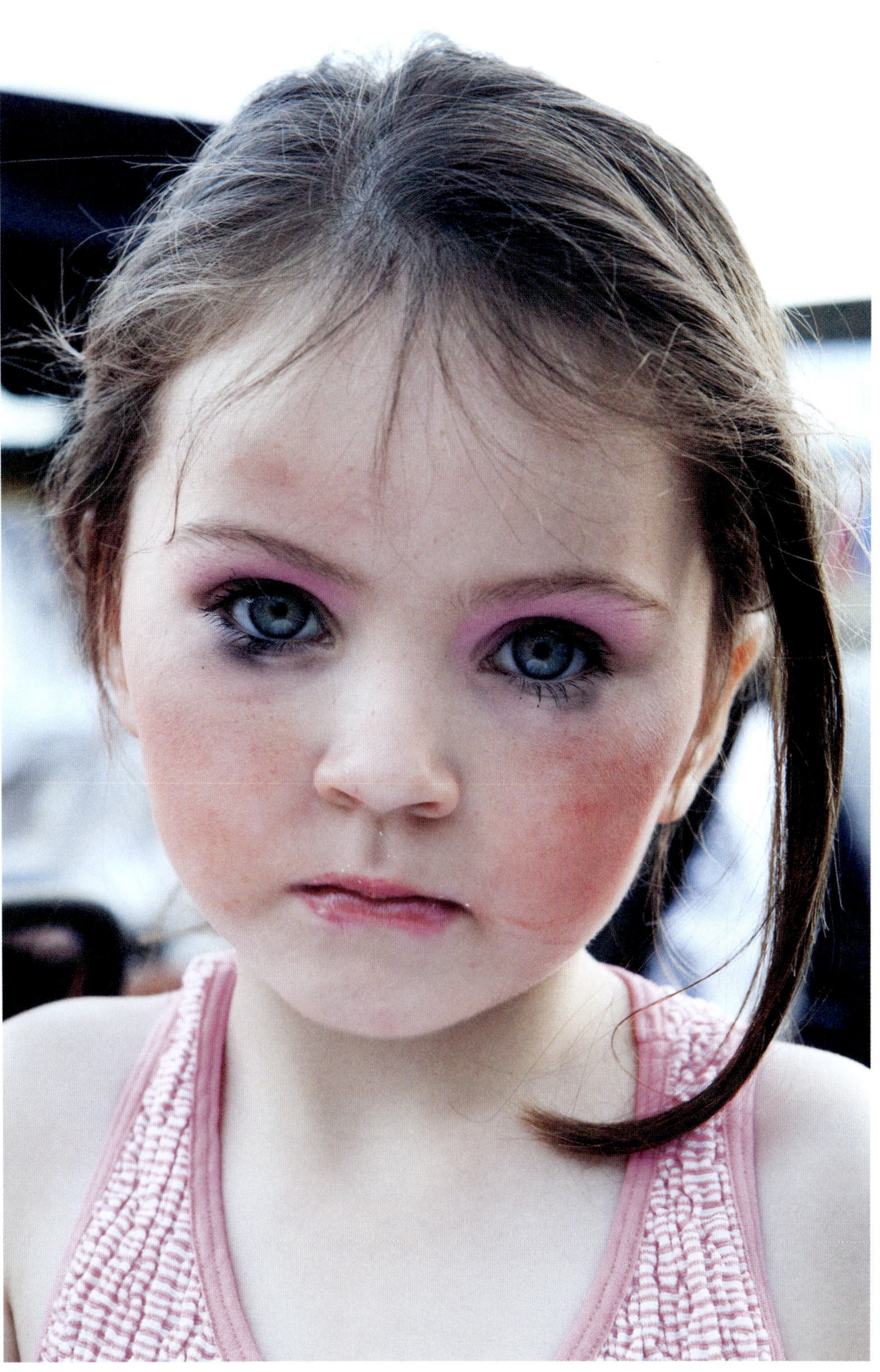

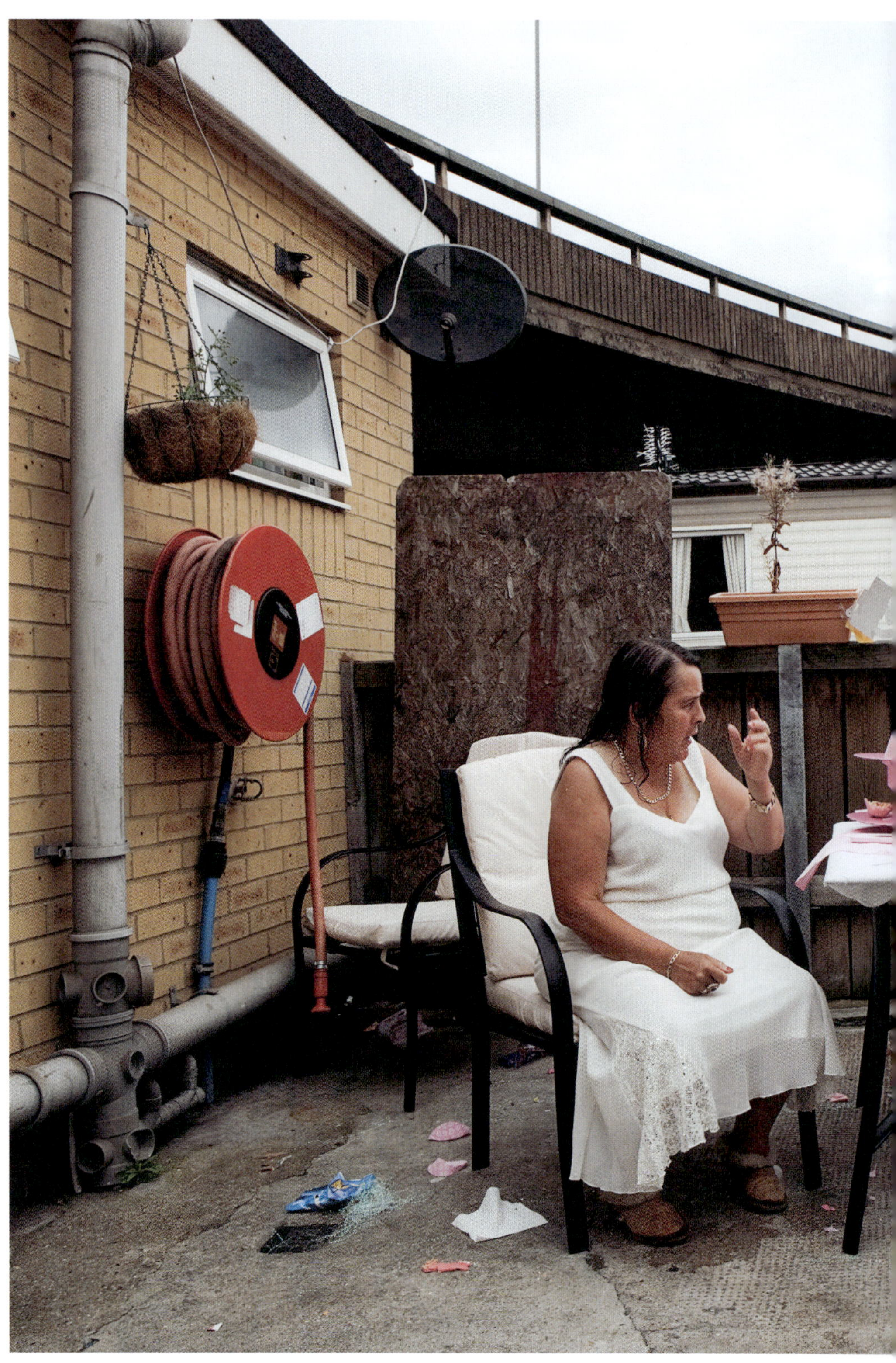

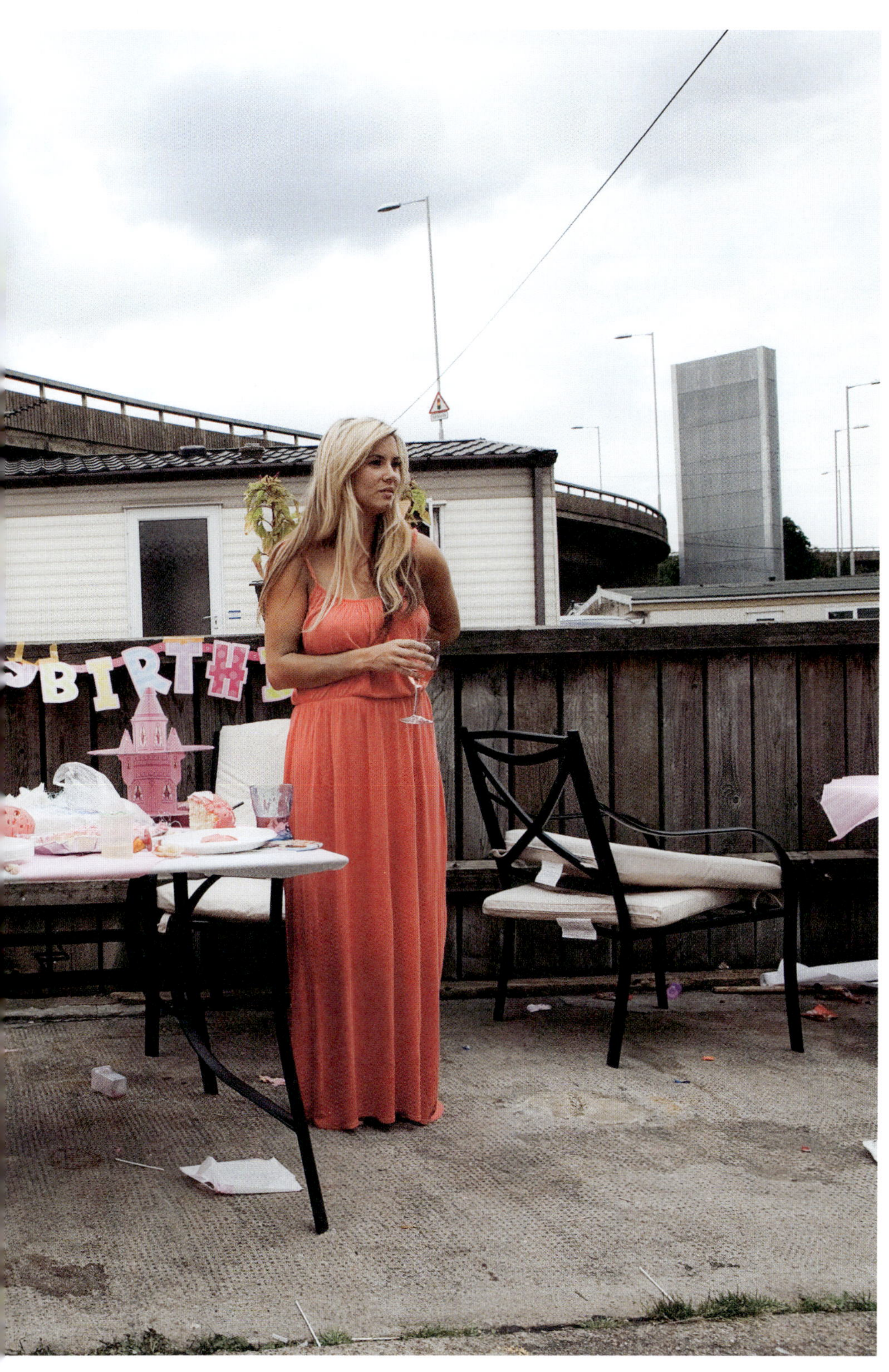
BIRTH

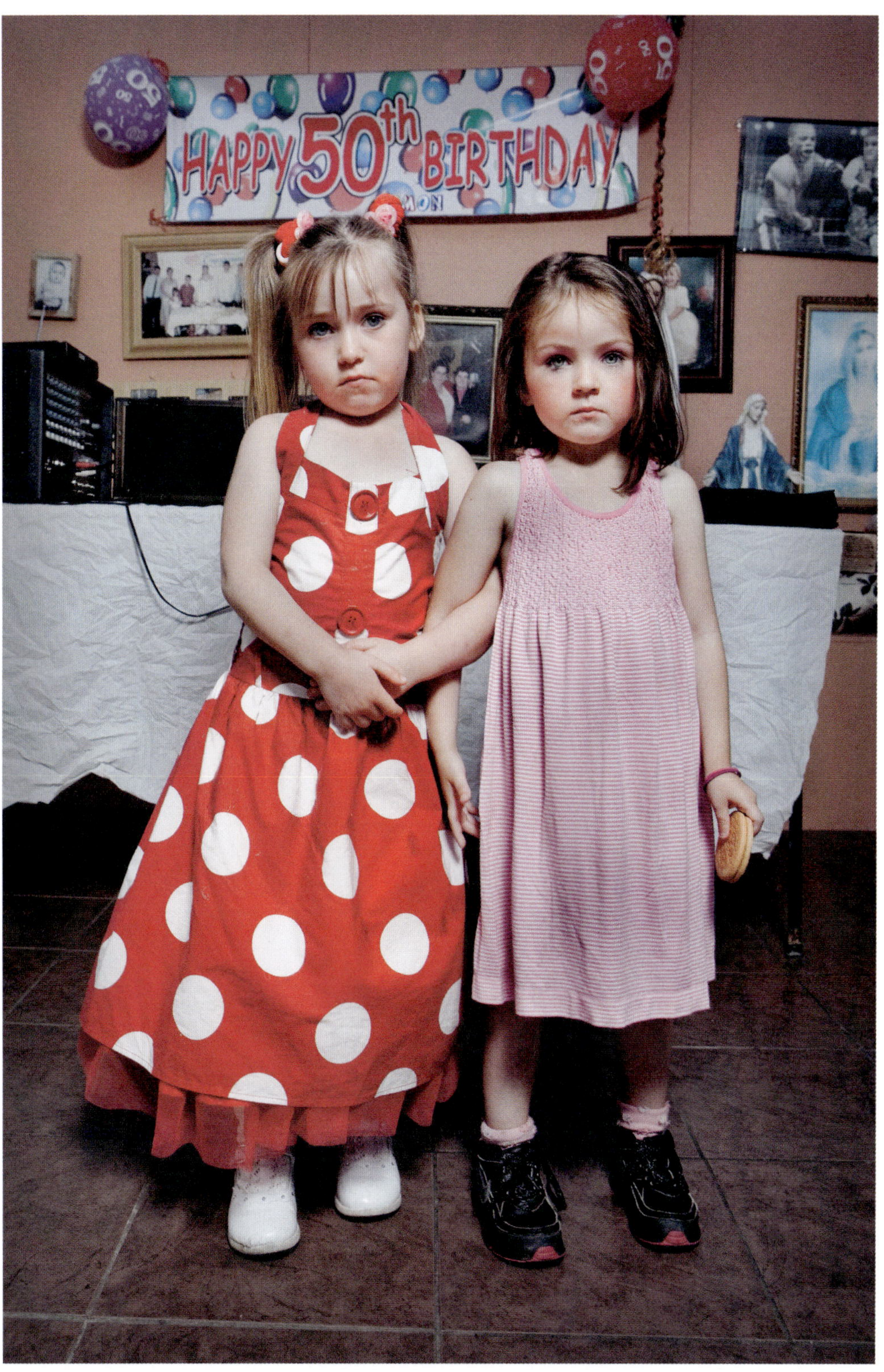

HAPPY 50th BIRTHDAY

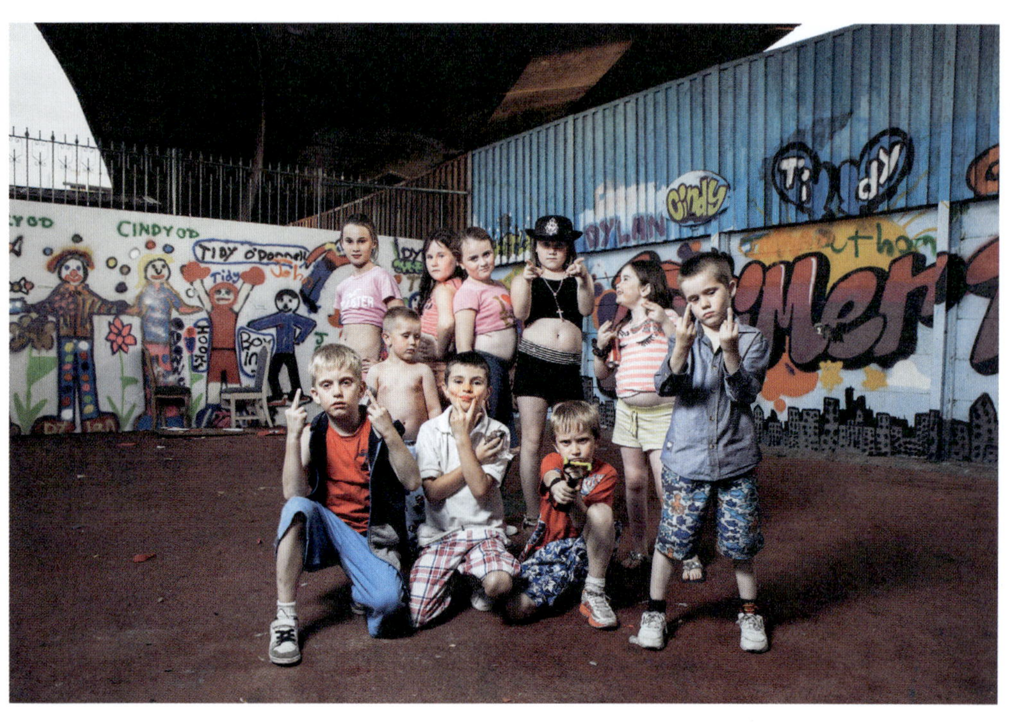

Sometimes kids would ask me what I had been doing recently and I would be about to tell them I had been playing with my kids in the garden. Then I would stop myself because I realised they had no garden, or green area at all, and that my life would sound very different from theirs.

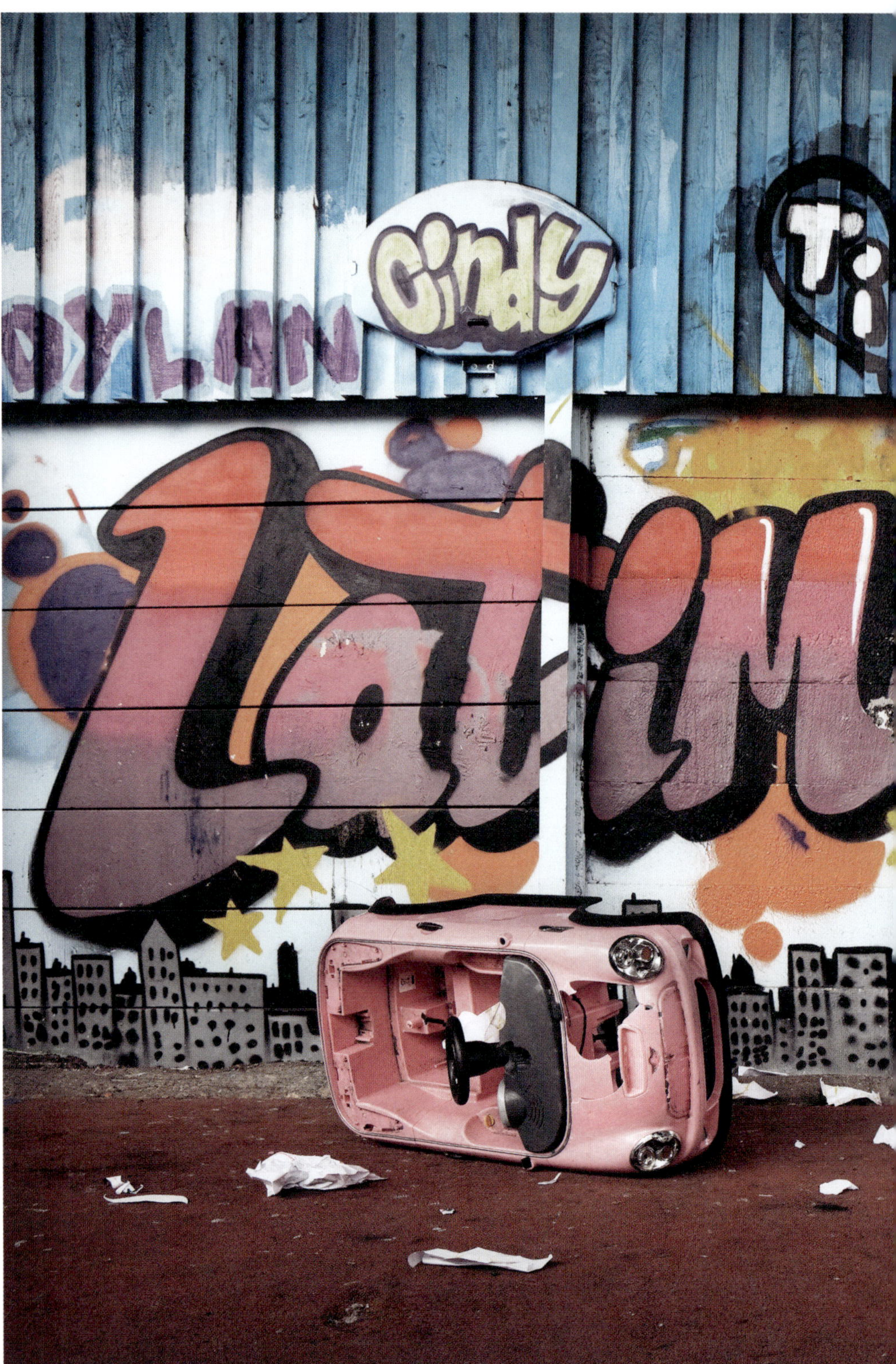

DYLAN
Cindy
Tï

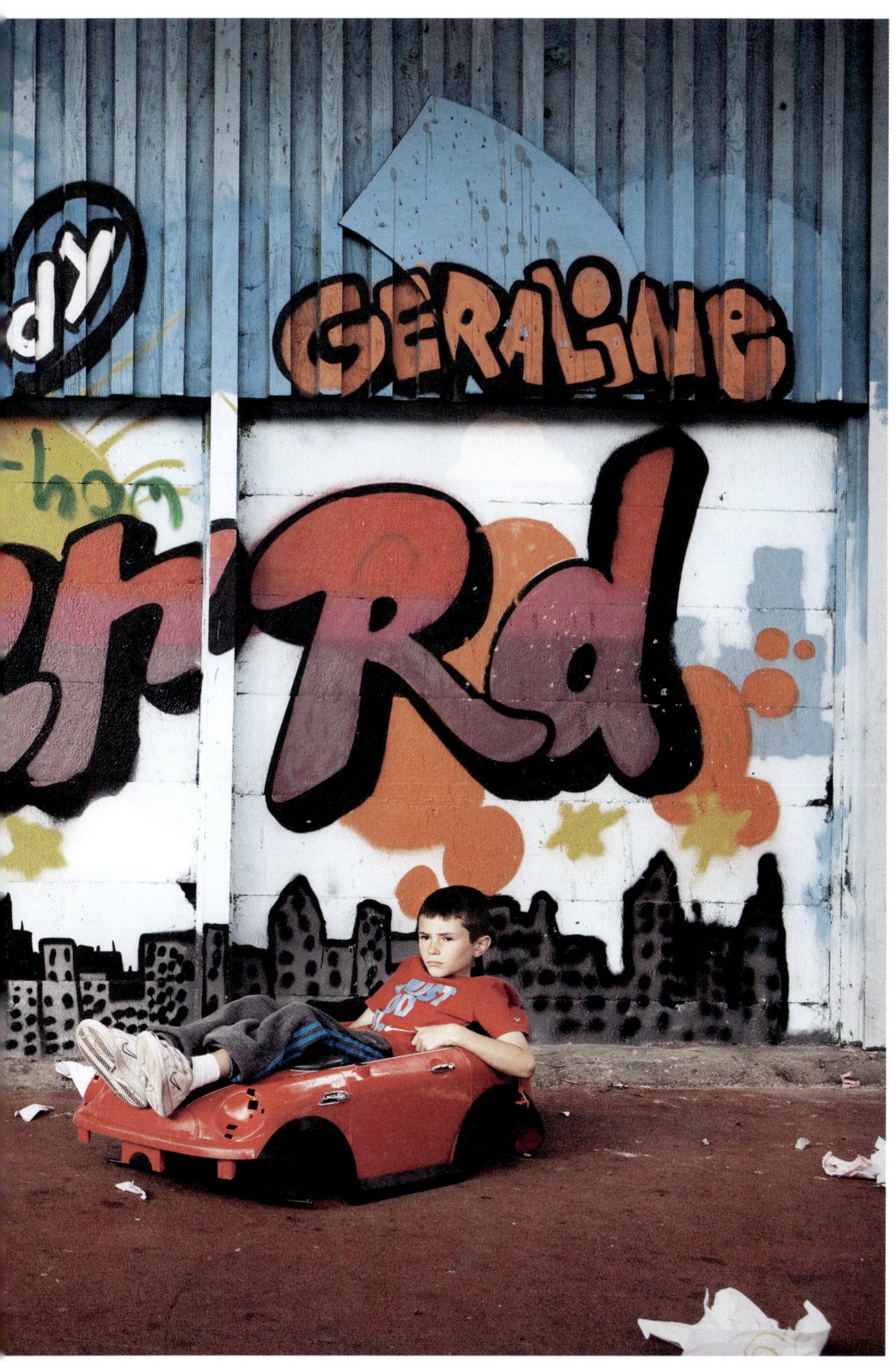
dY
GERALINE

The Travellers had their parties in local pubs, although only certain places would accept them. Many said no as soon as they realised that Travellers were trying to book. It didn't matter if it was for a birthday, wedding, or first communion, if they knew it was Travellers, they would be fully booked.

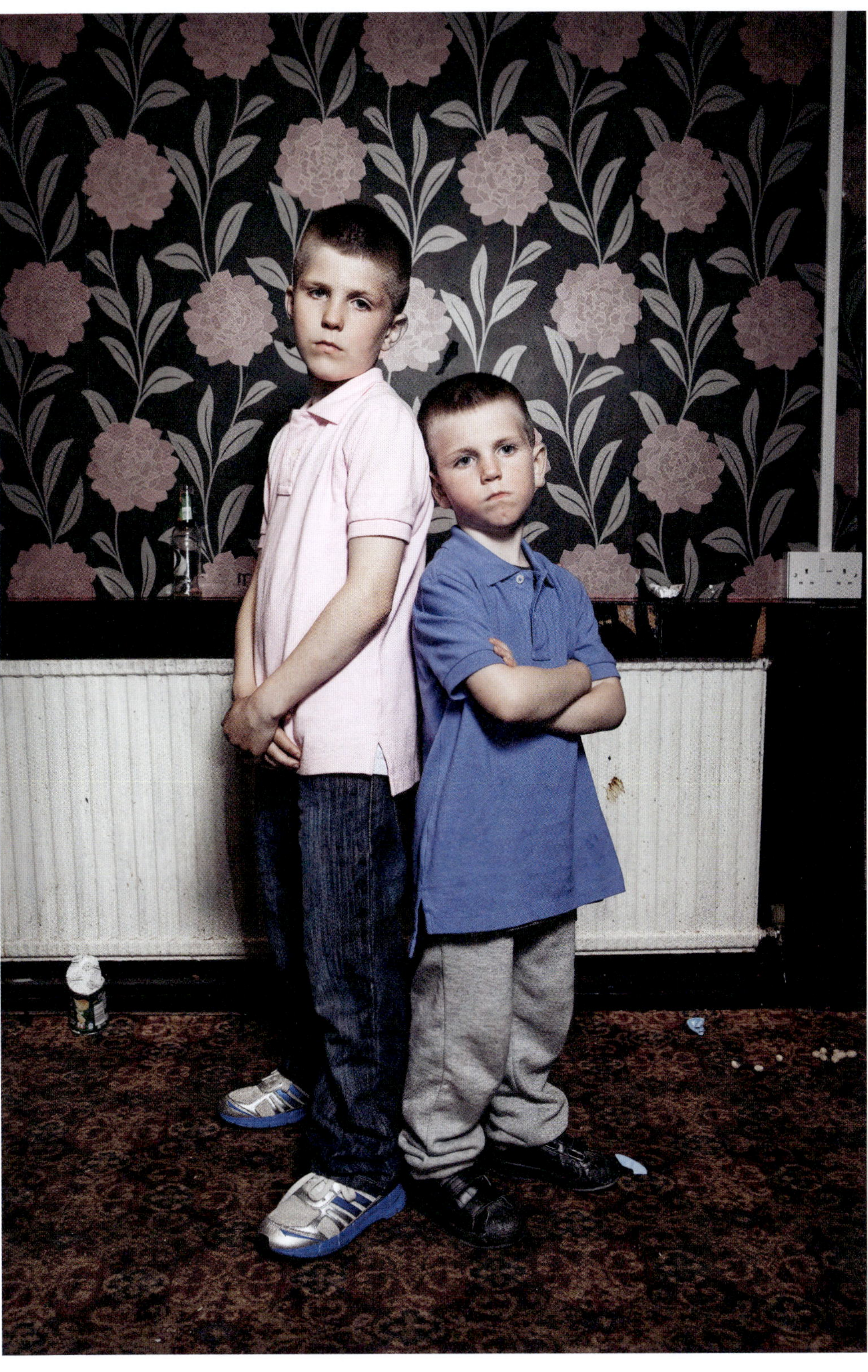

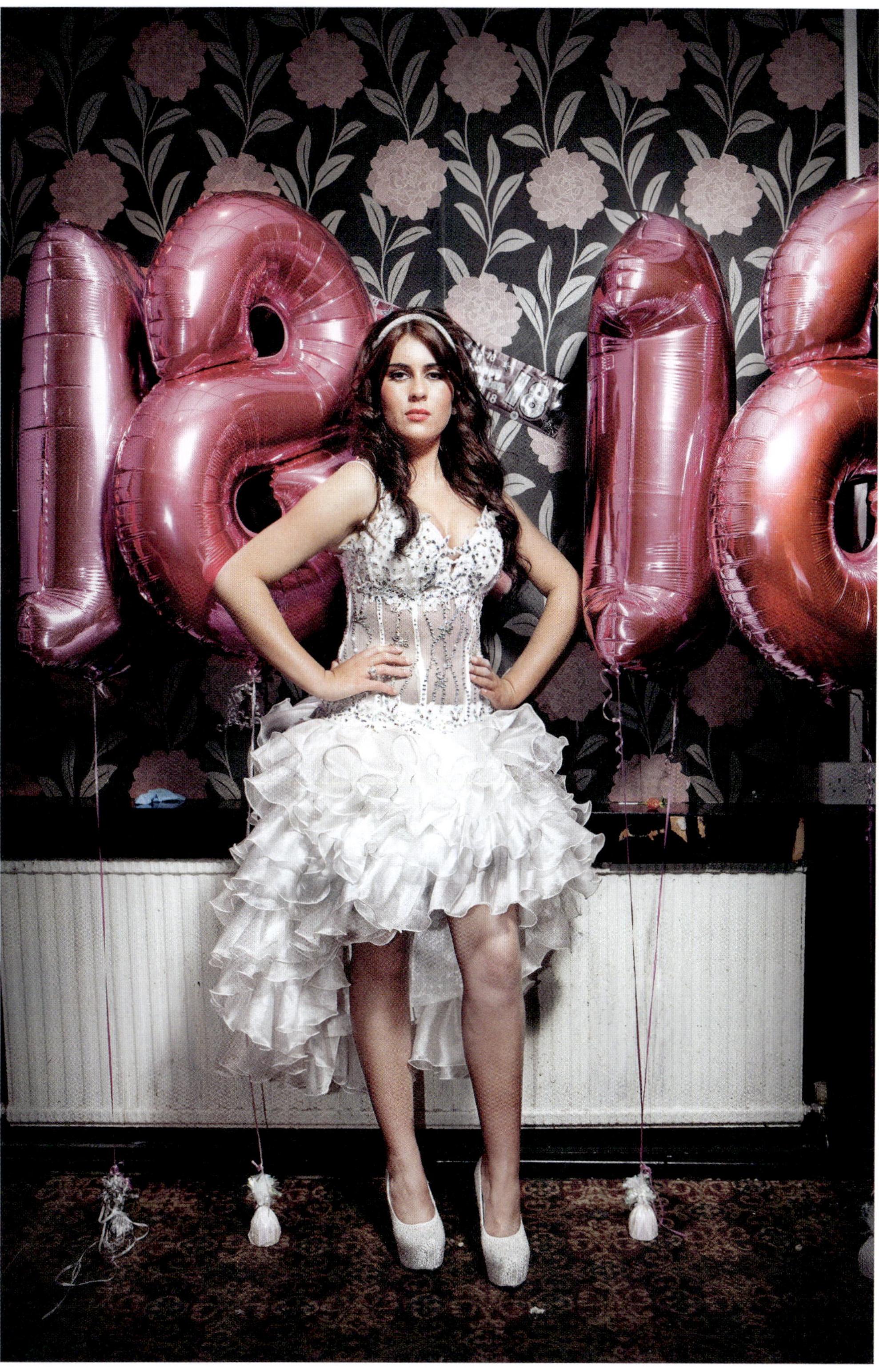

The Travellers get married quite young and have large families, but for many Catholics this is quite normal. They have traditional marriages in which the wife stays at home and the husband goes out to work. Travellers are expected to marry once and divorce is frowned upon.

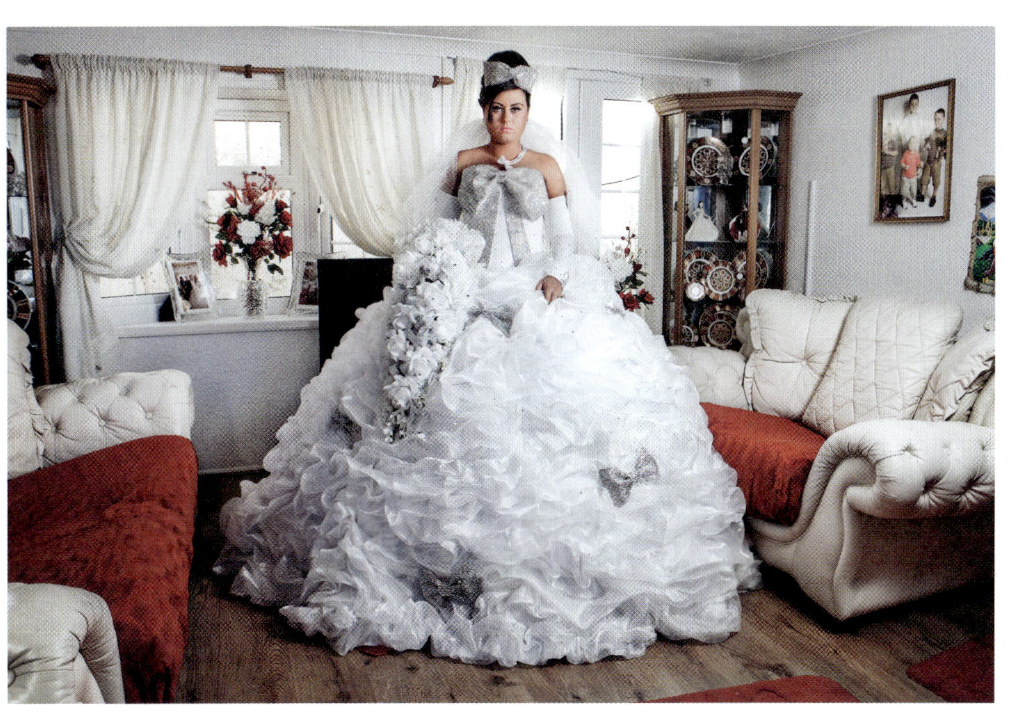

The Travellers don't smile for the camera like us Gorgers (non-Traveller folk). They smile when they are happy and don't feel the need to put on a fake smile for the photographer.

So sometimes you could tell if someone had not lived with the Travellers for a long time, as they would instantly smile when I raised the camera.

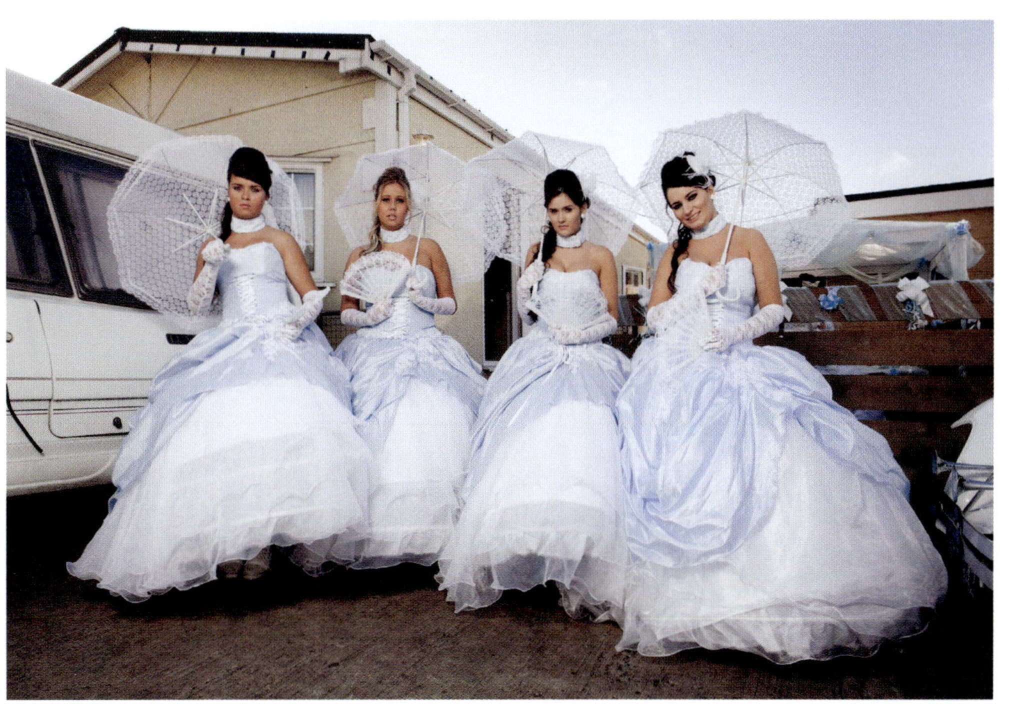

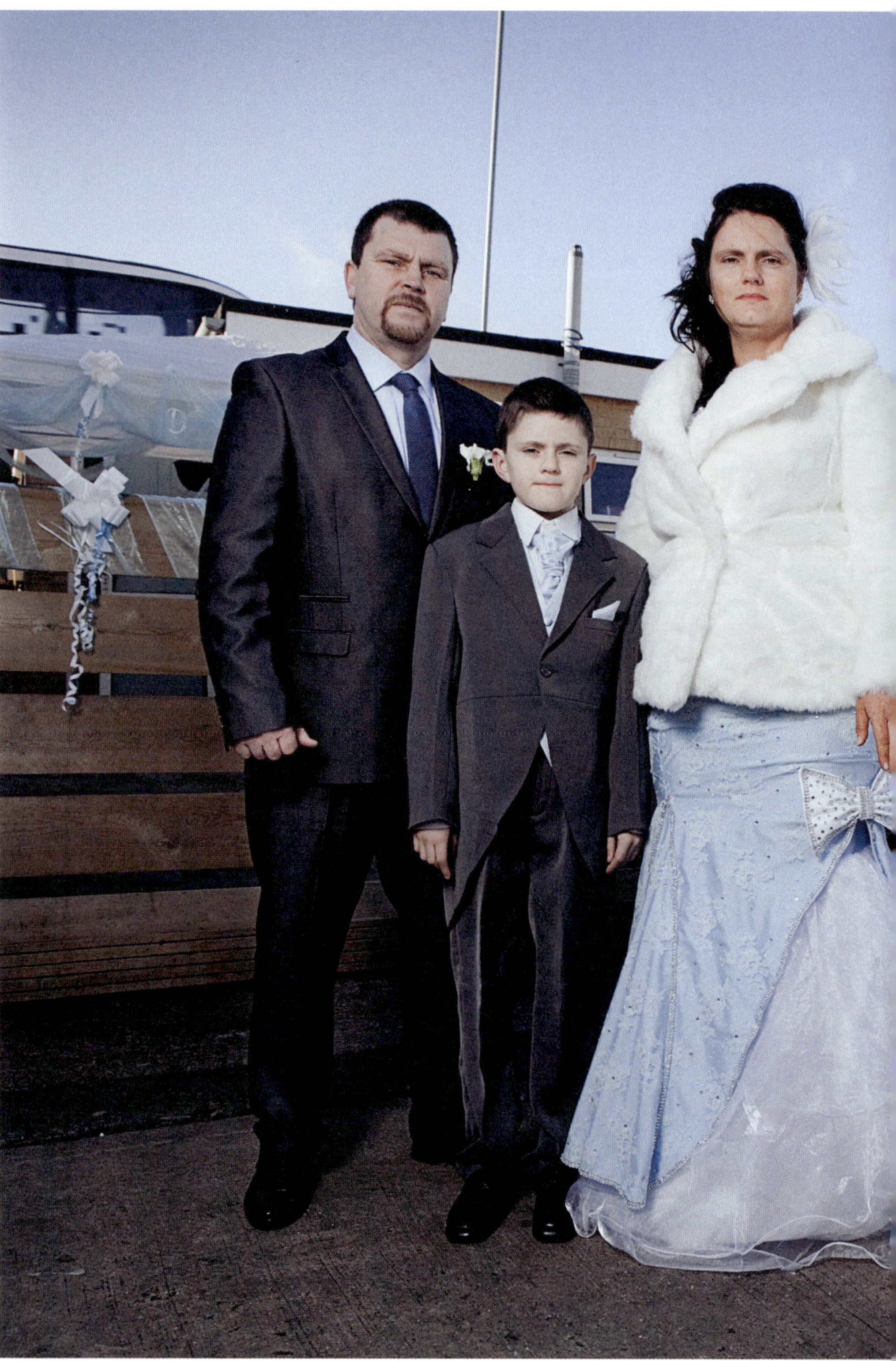

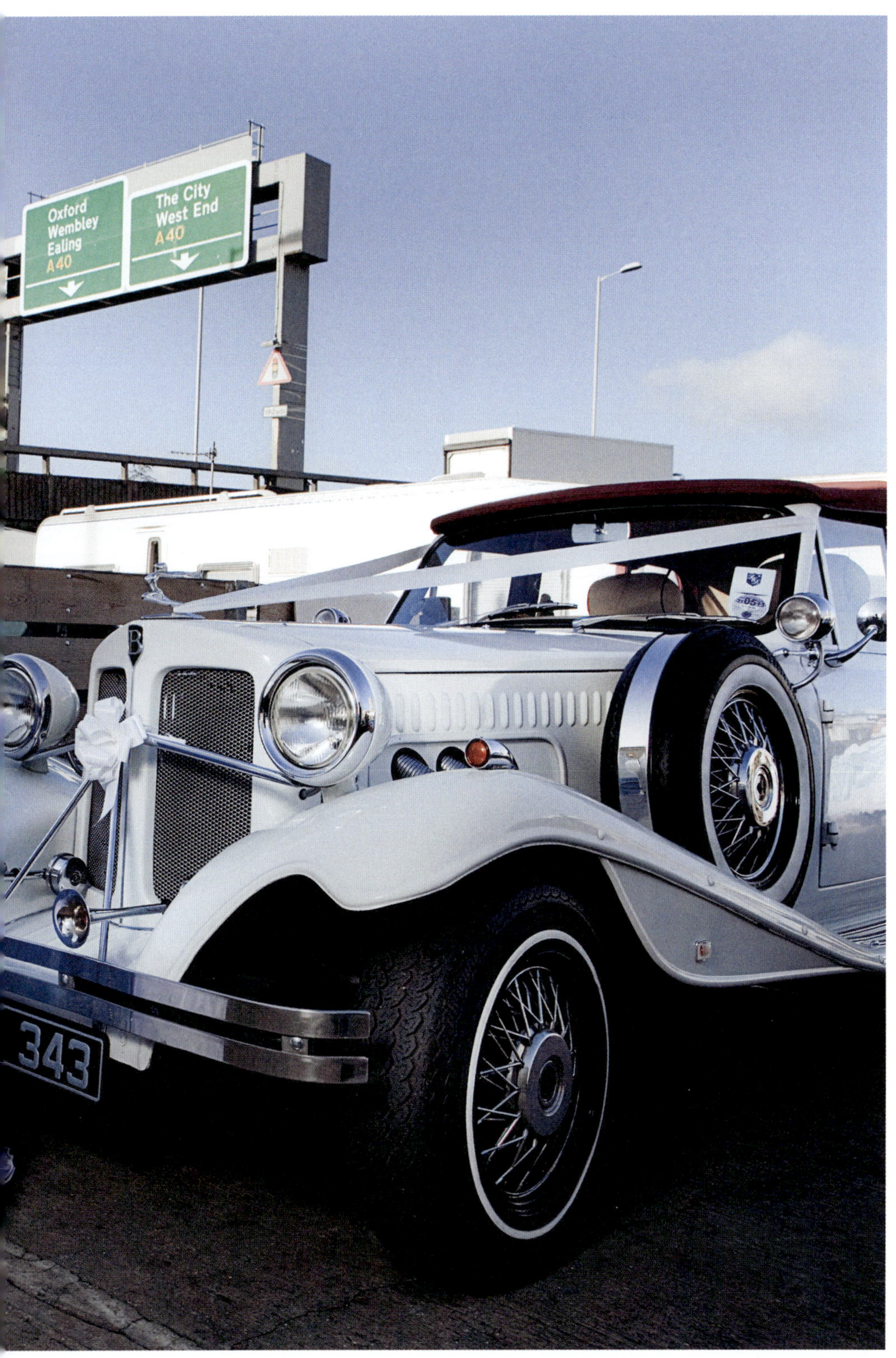

Oxford
Wembley
Ealing
A40
The City
West End
A40
343

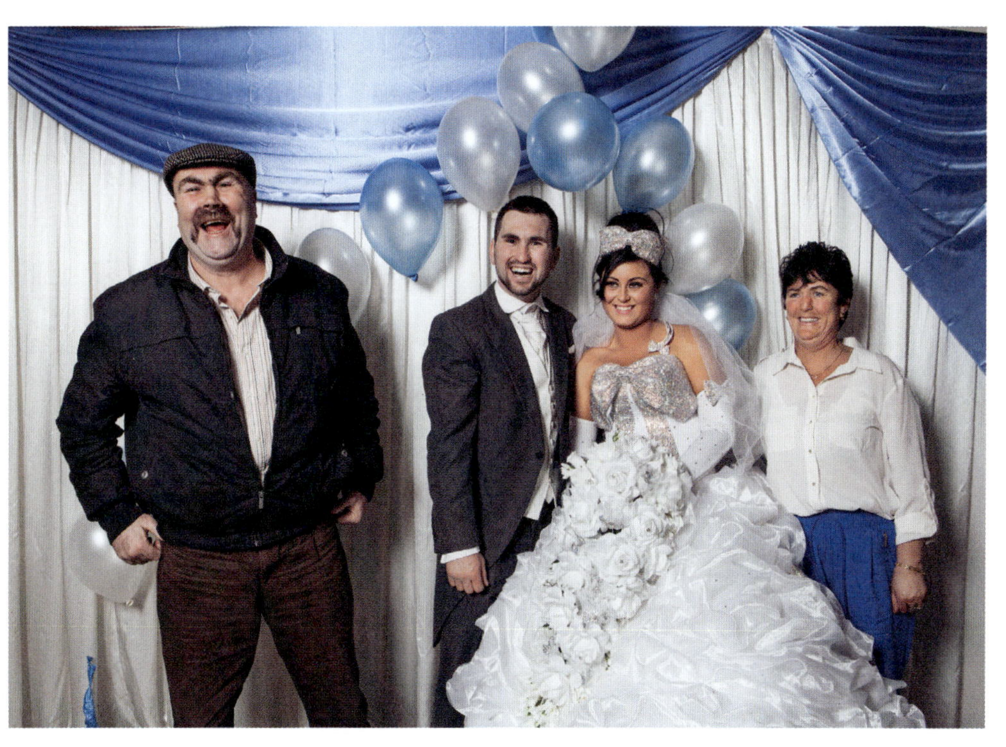

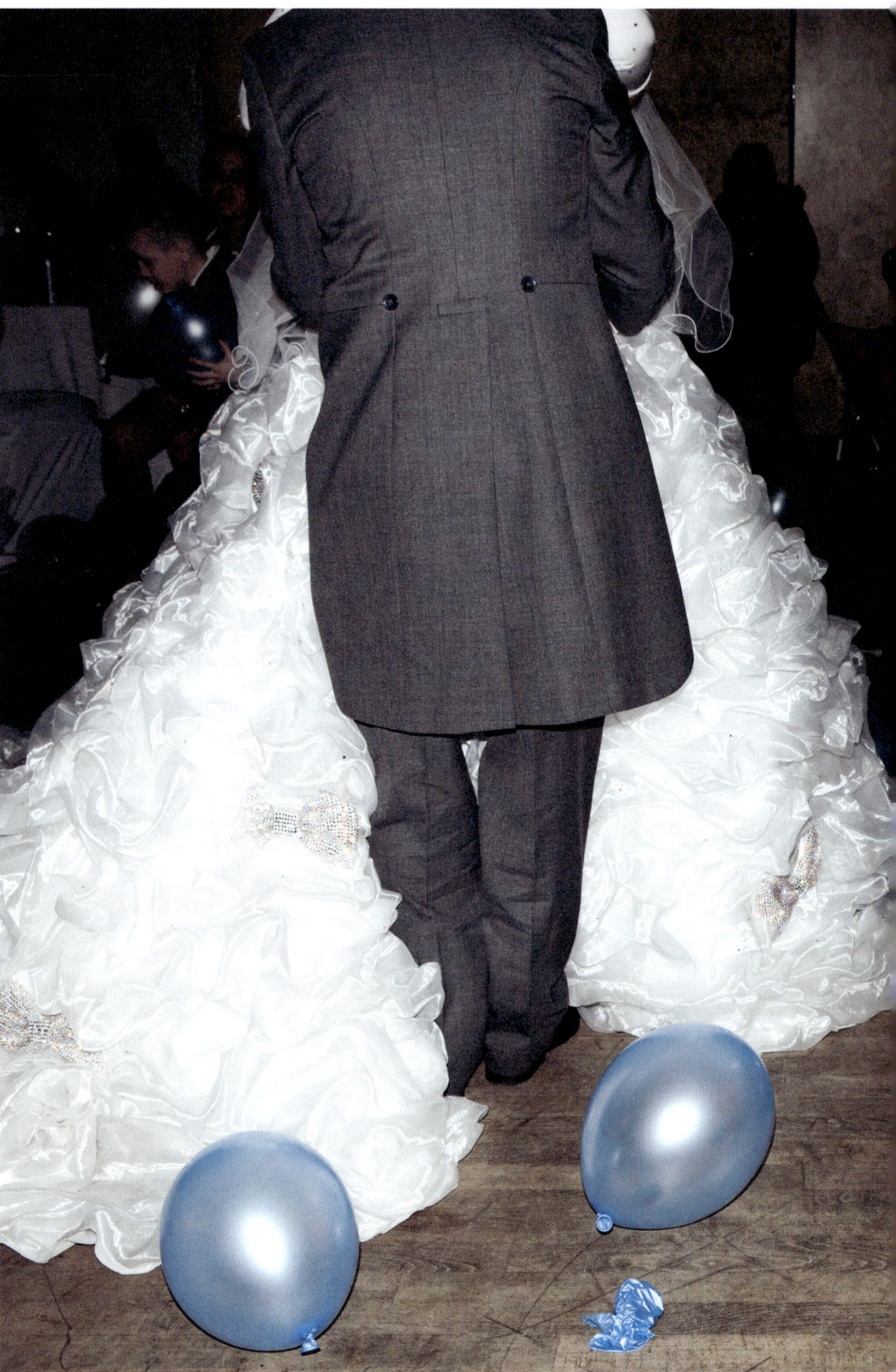

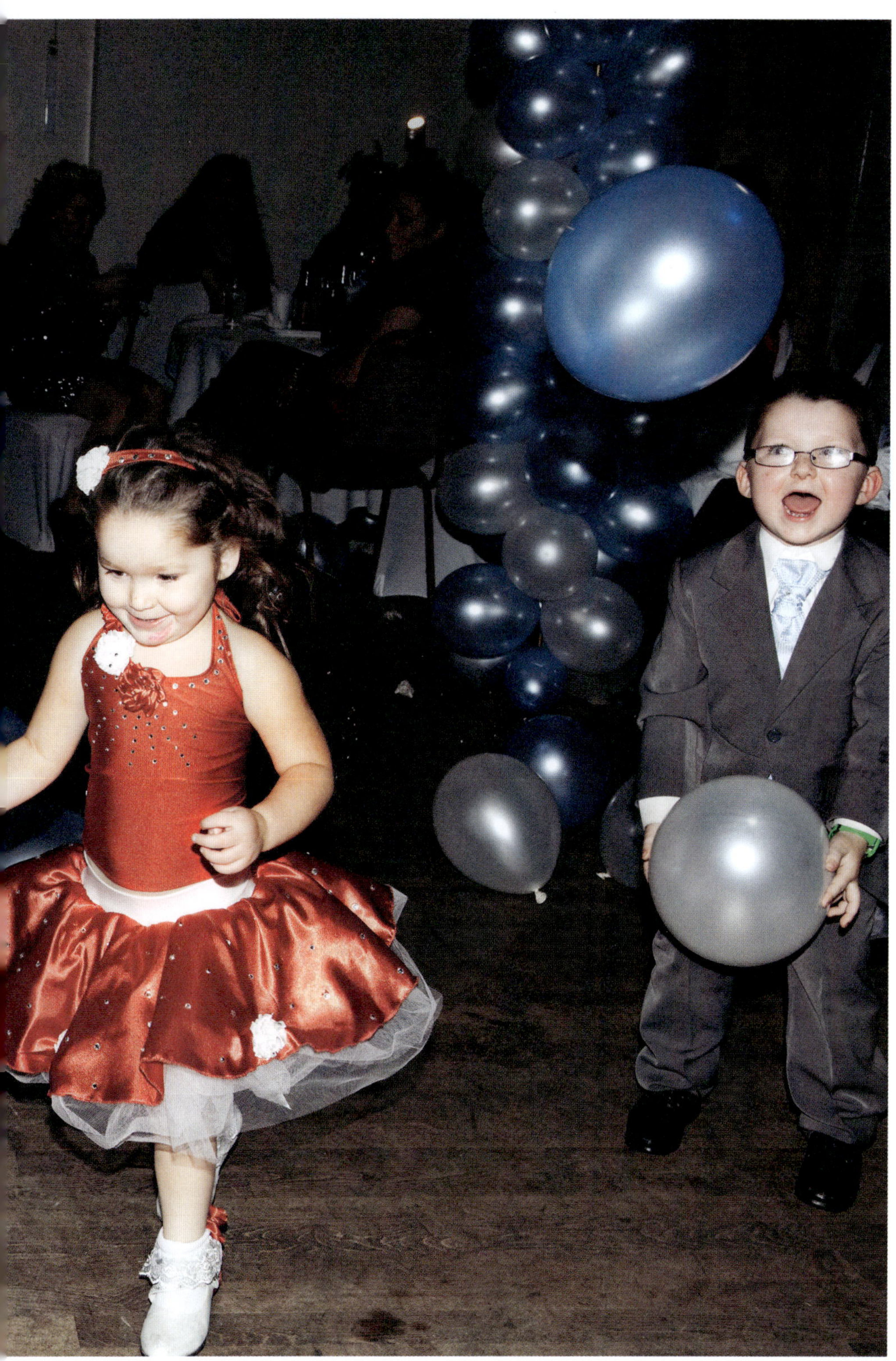

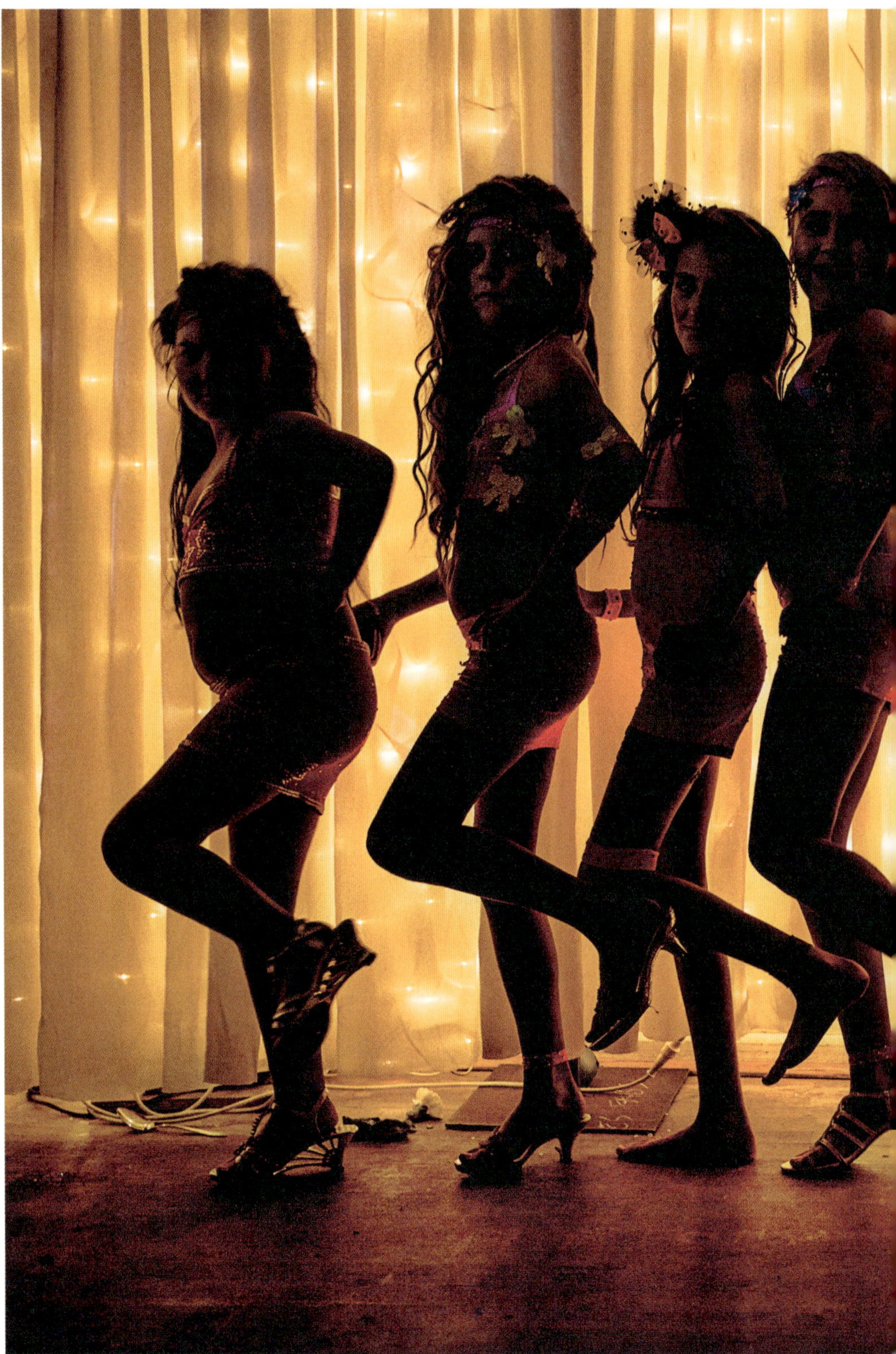

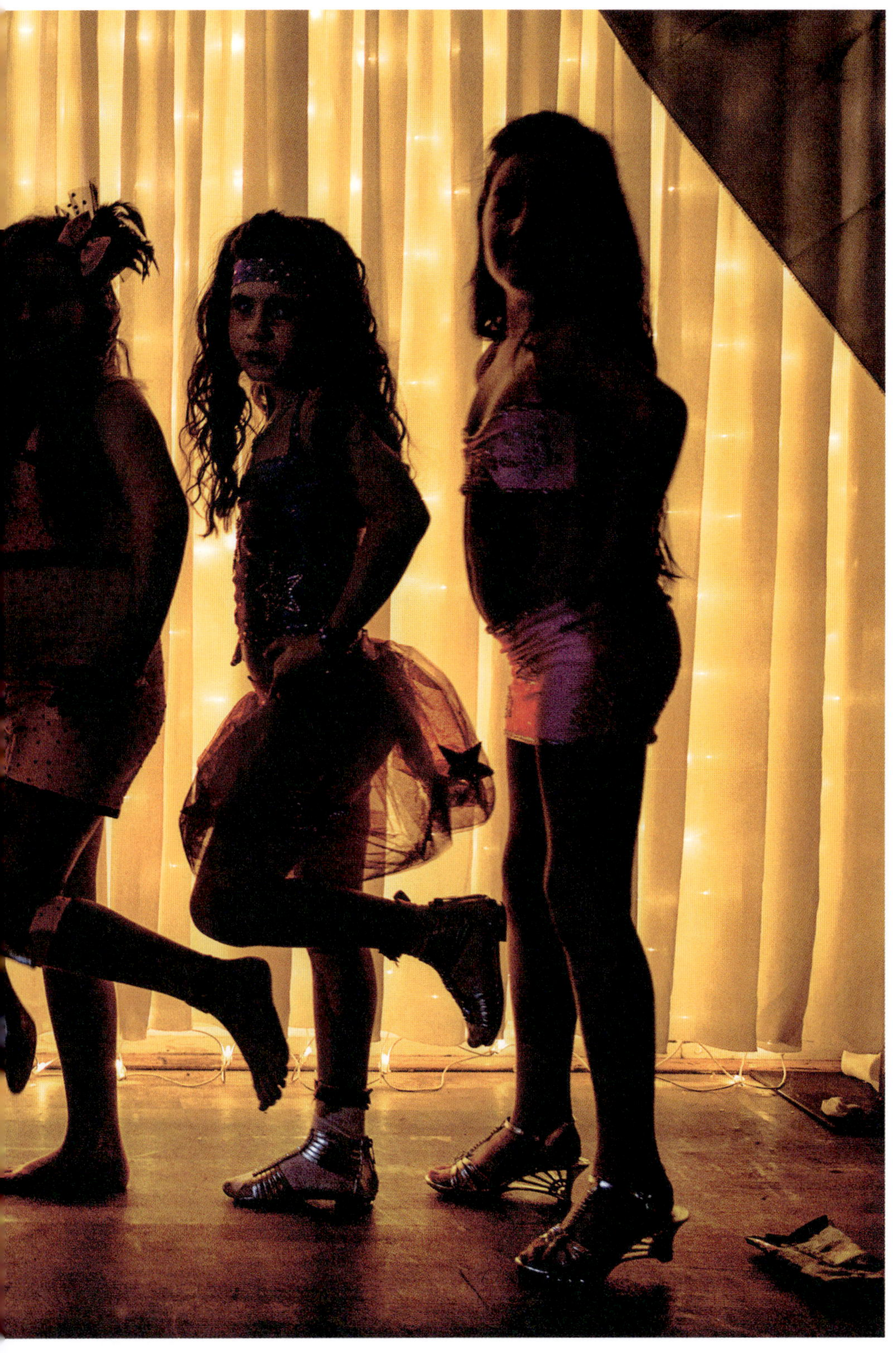

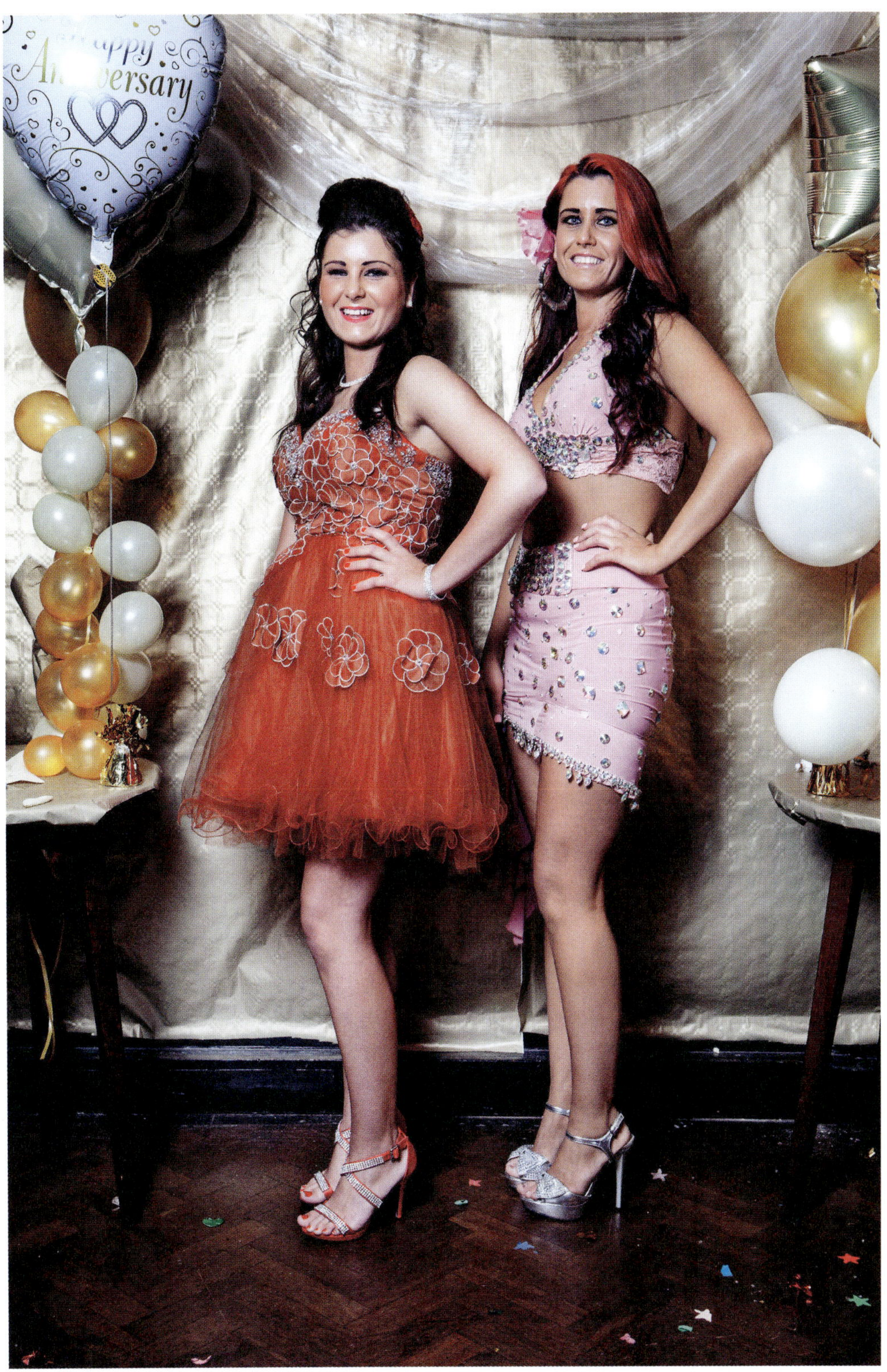

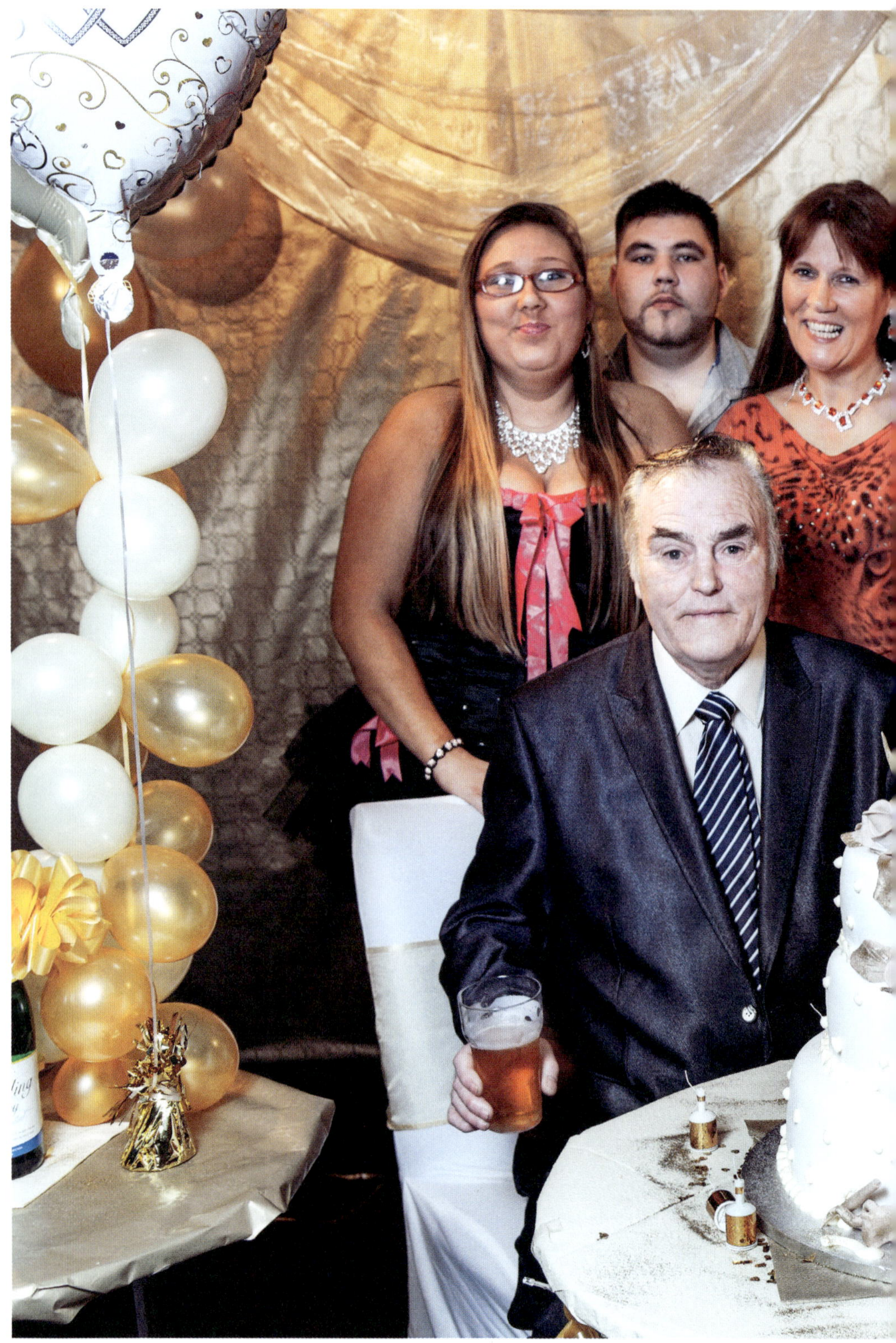

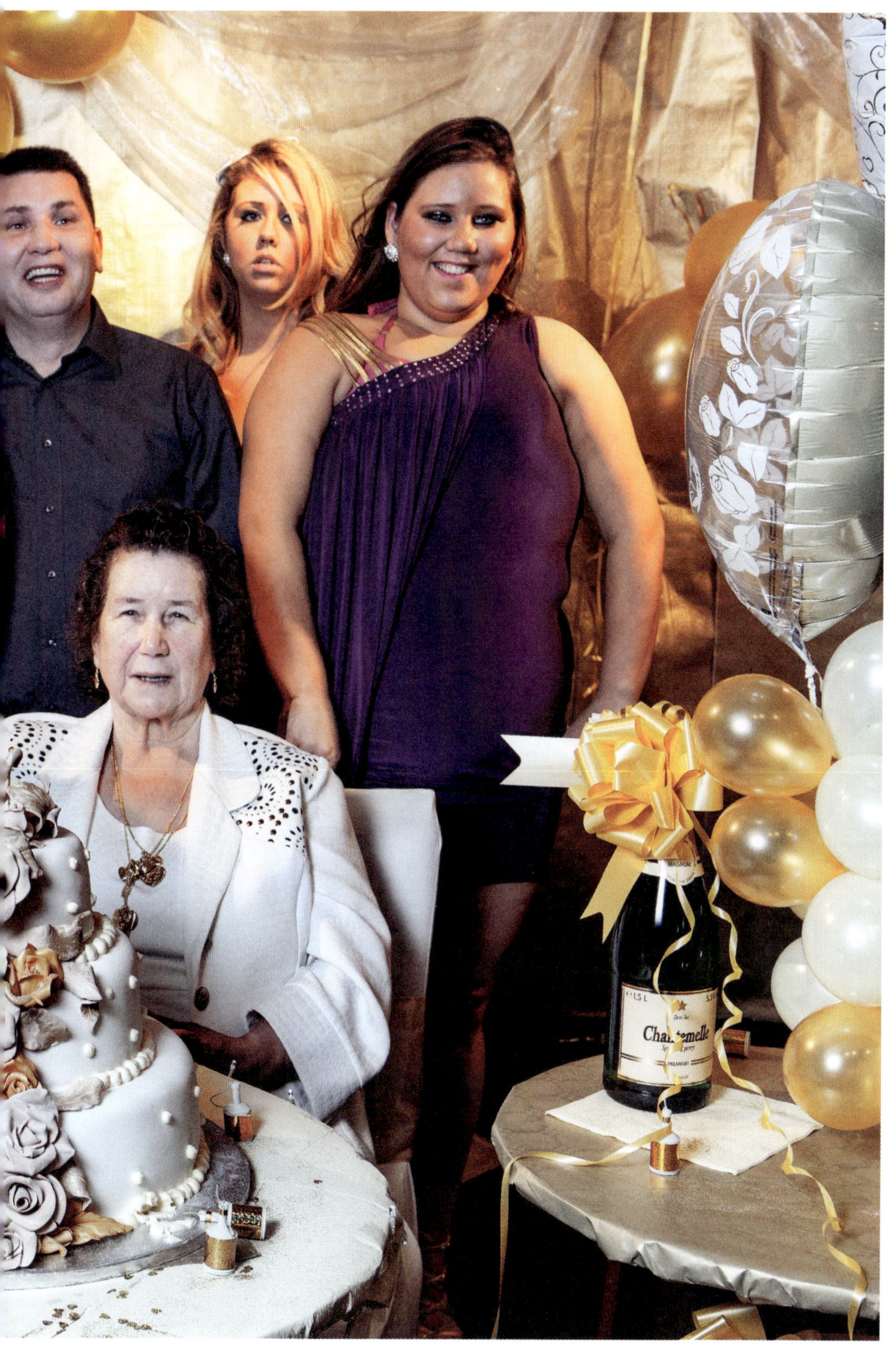

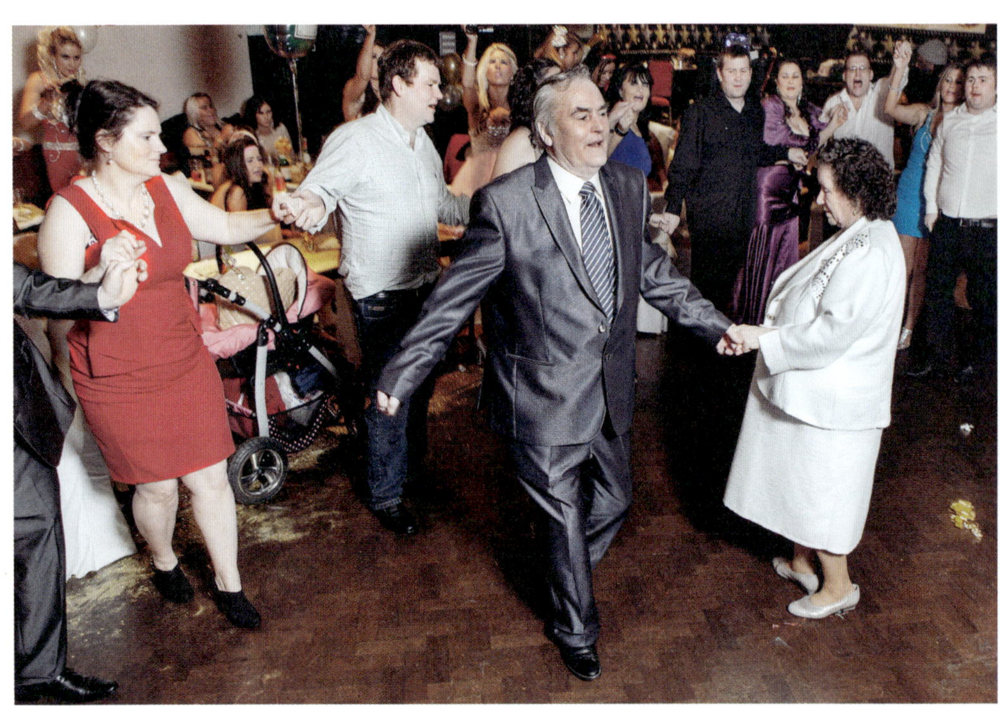

It was wonderful to see Pat's mum and dad dancing at their 50th wedding anniversary. As I took this photo and watched four generations enjoying each other's company, the sense of family was overwhelming. They were all so connected and involved with each other's lives that I thought perhaps we Gorgers could learn a lot from them.

However, with so many families living closely together and with more children growing up, this has gradually led to overcrowding. The Travellers point out that the site is rented from the council and they pay a decent amount of money. They don't get the place for free, as some locals seem to think.

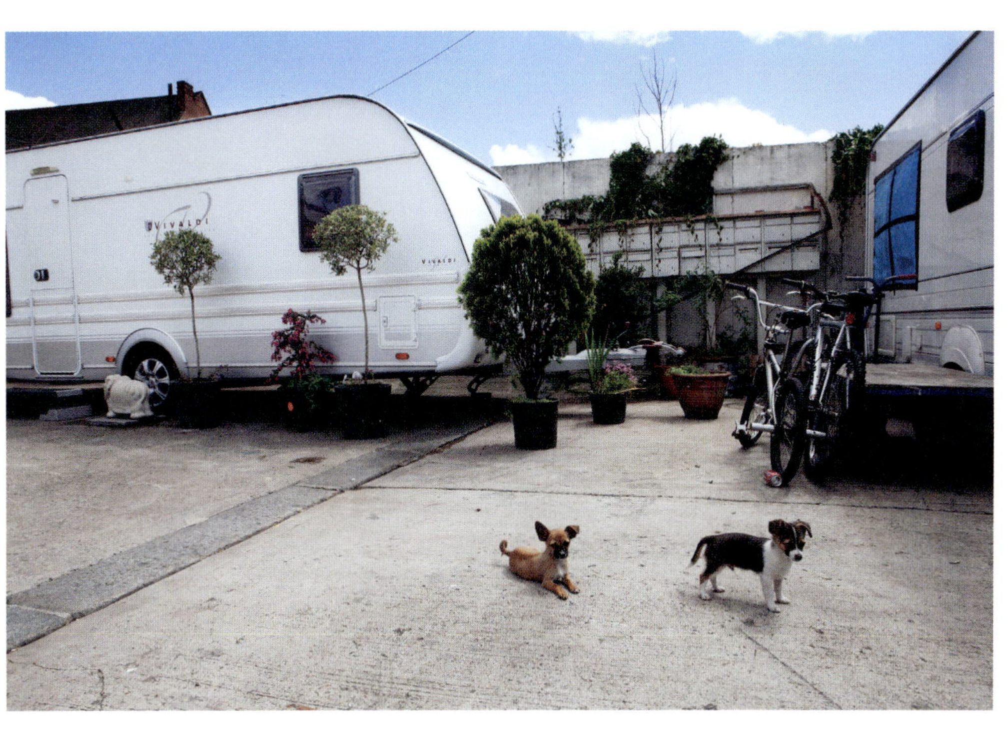

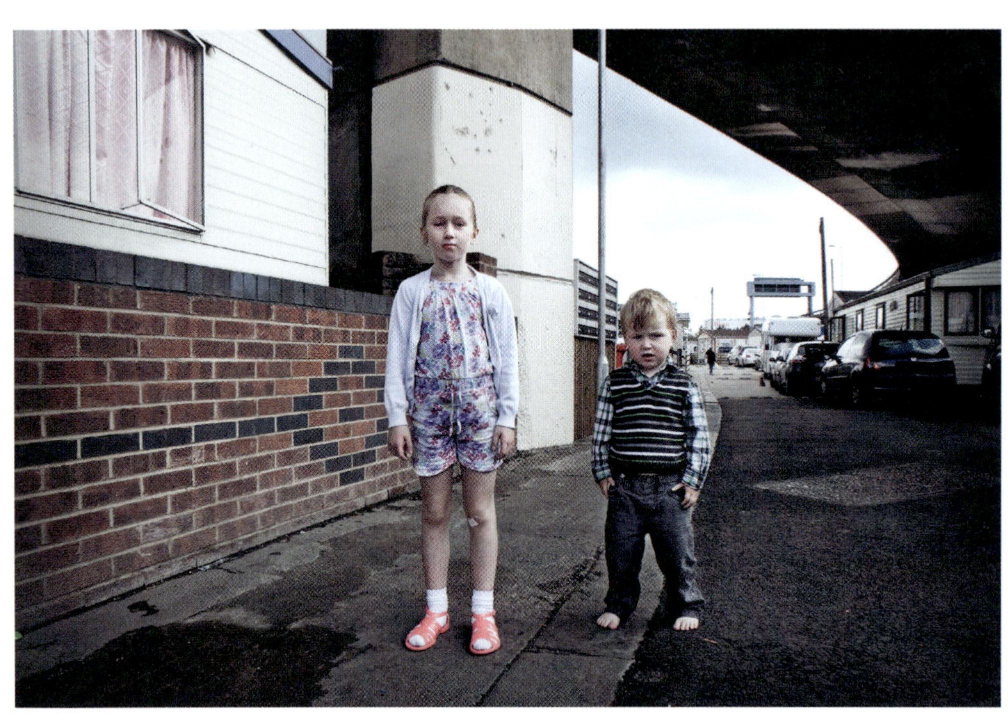

The Traveller site was made official decades ago when the land was worth nothing. But now, great amounts of redevelopment are going on around them and the Travellers are under pressure by the local council to move on. They don't want to go unless they can stay together and so far, they are resisting.

The horse-riding school which the Travellers used to use and keep horses in has now closed after many years. The land is due to be redeveloped.

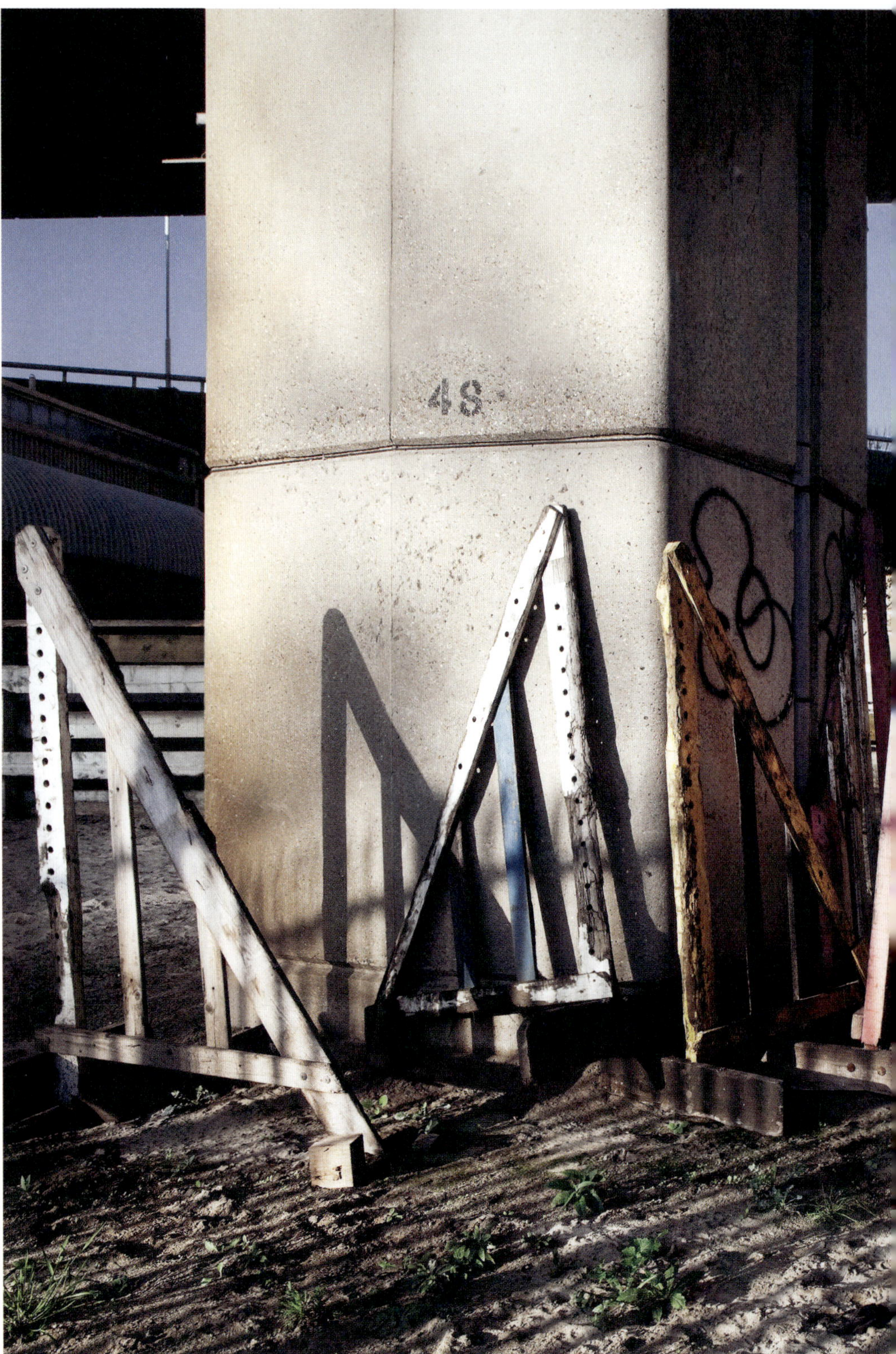
48

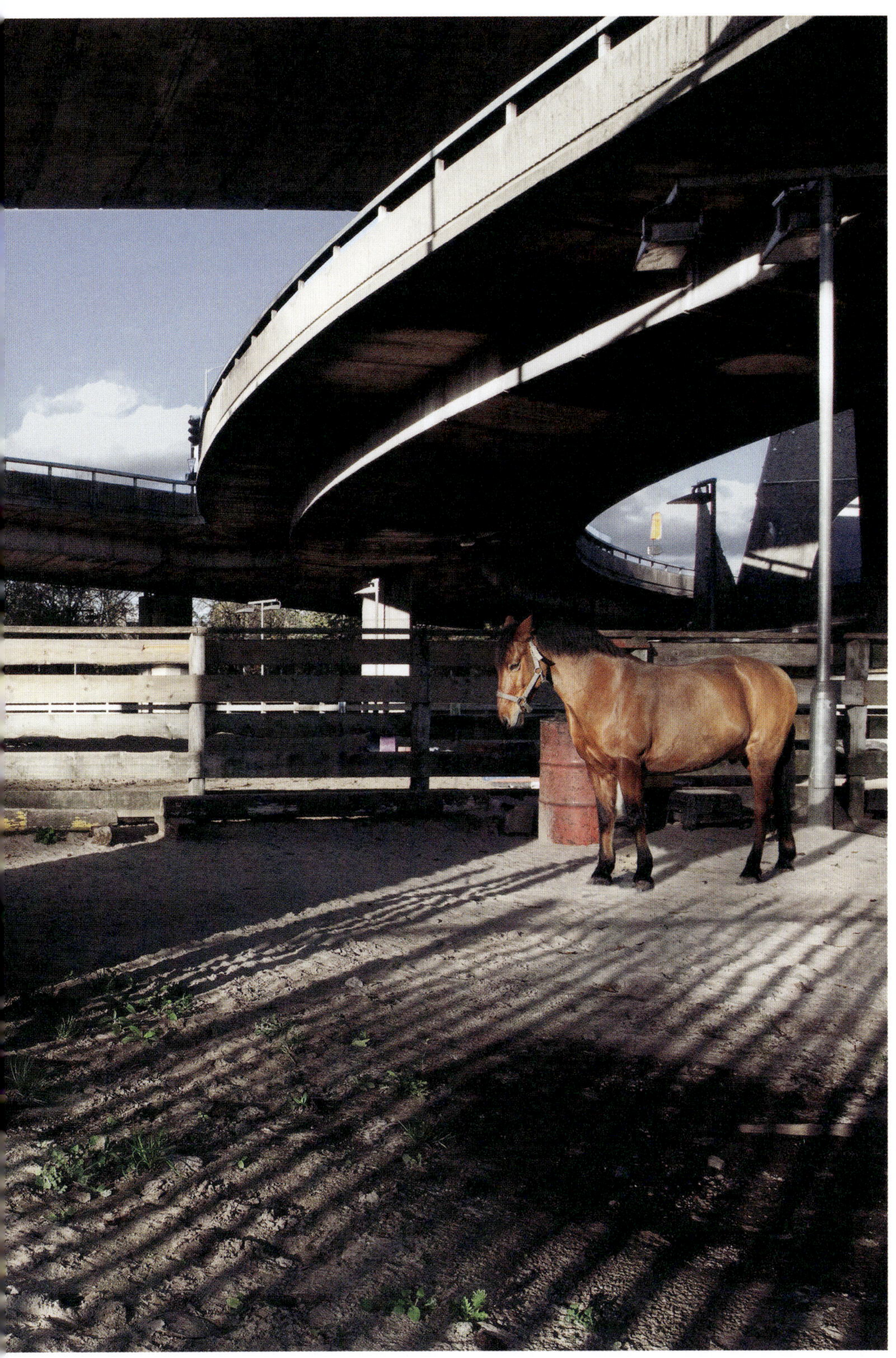

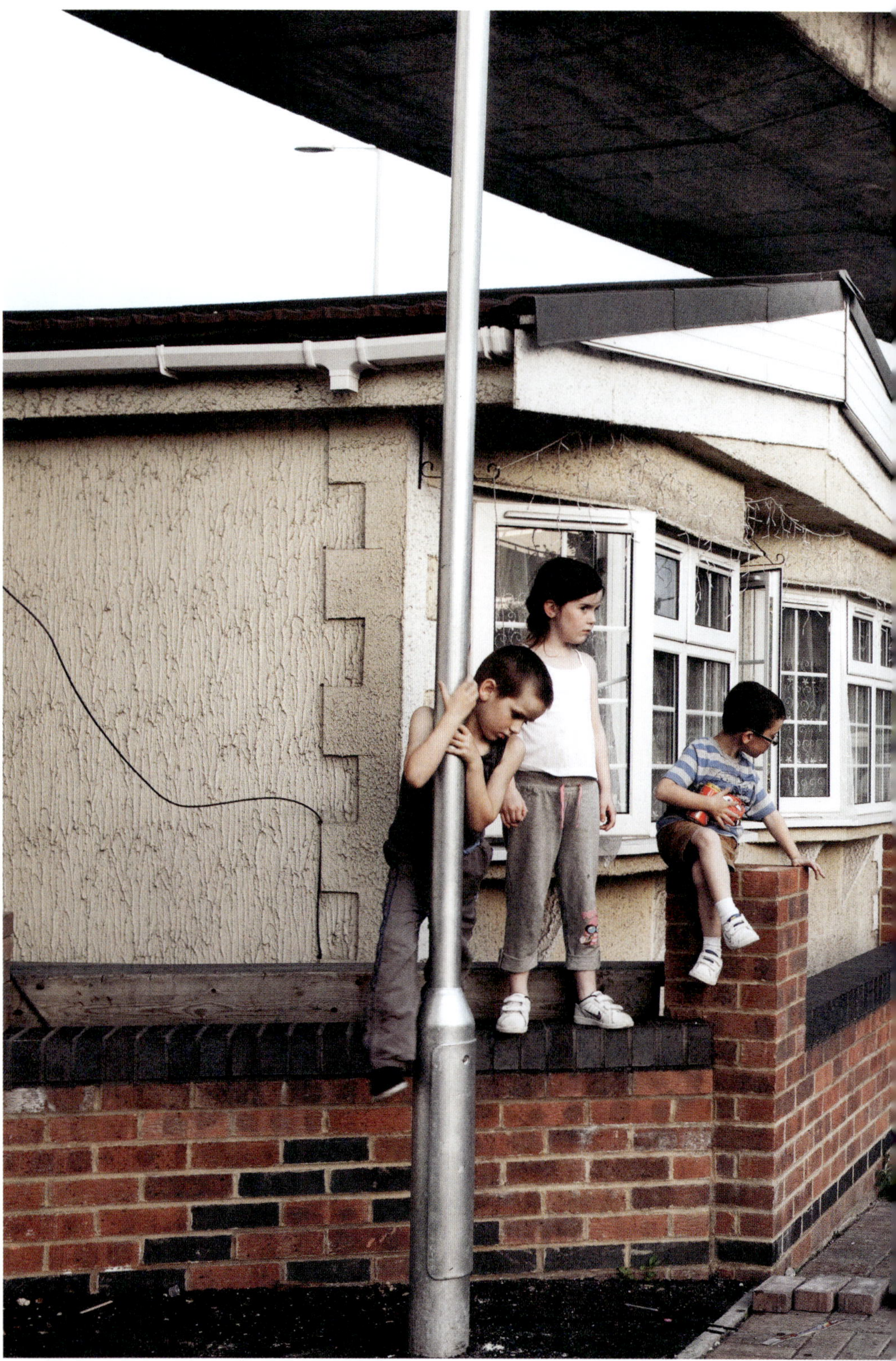

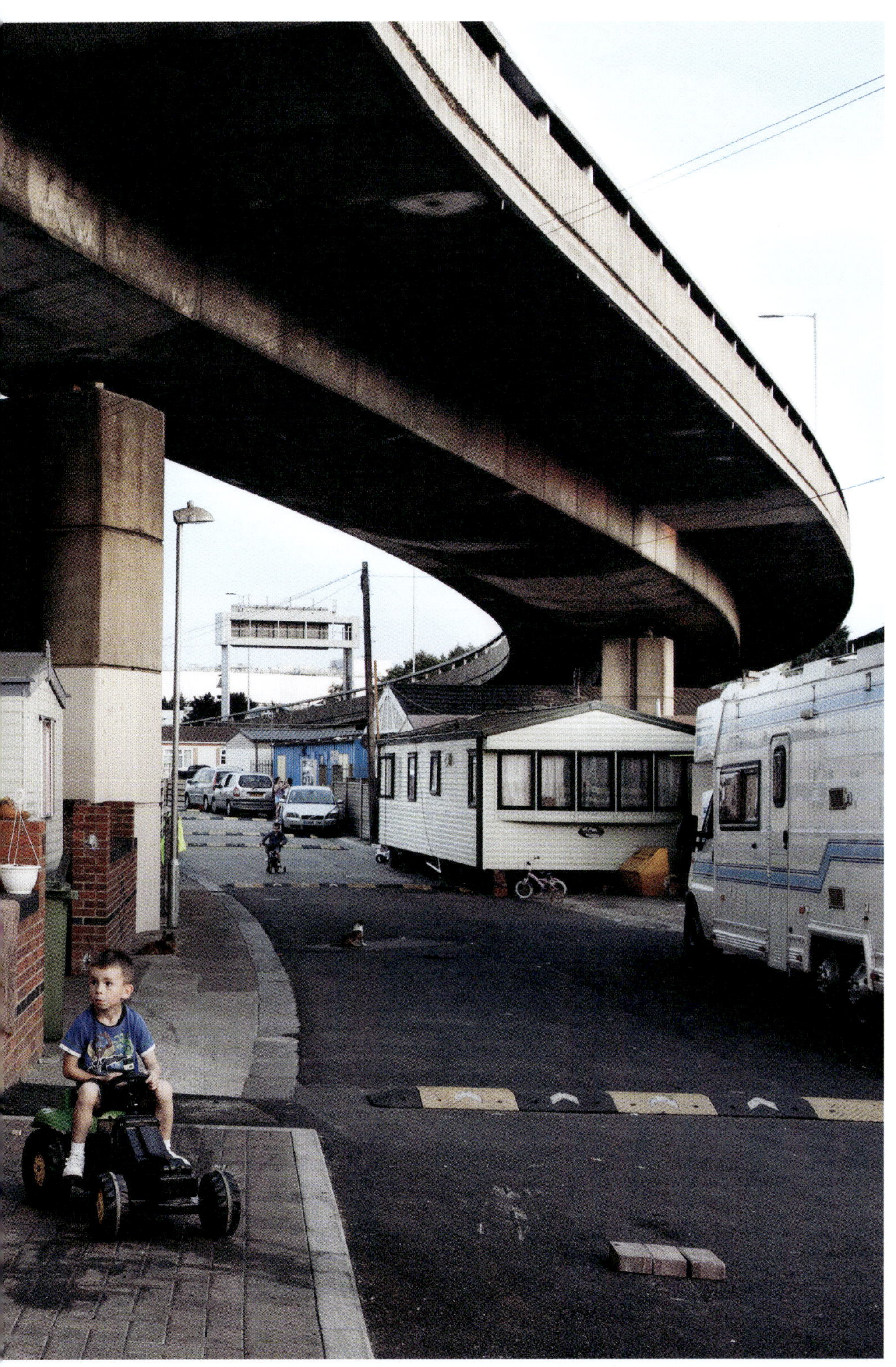

After photographing the Travellers for about a year, I had got to know them well. It seems that their old way of life is under threat. They are under great pressure to conform.

Some people believe that the attitude shown towards Travellers in this country is the last acceptable form of racism. I, for one, feel privileged to have spent time with the Westway Travellers and I wish them well for the future. Who knows what will happen to the site in the years to come, but I hope we make room for them and that their community flourishes.

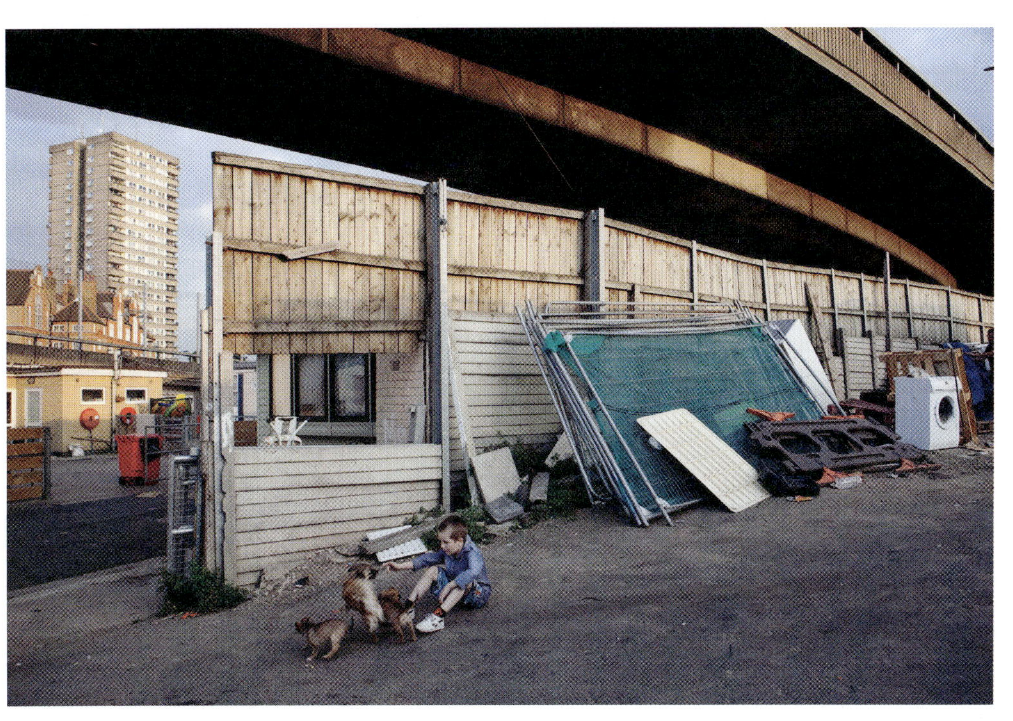

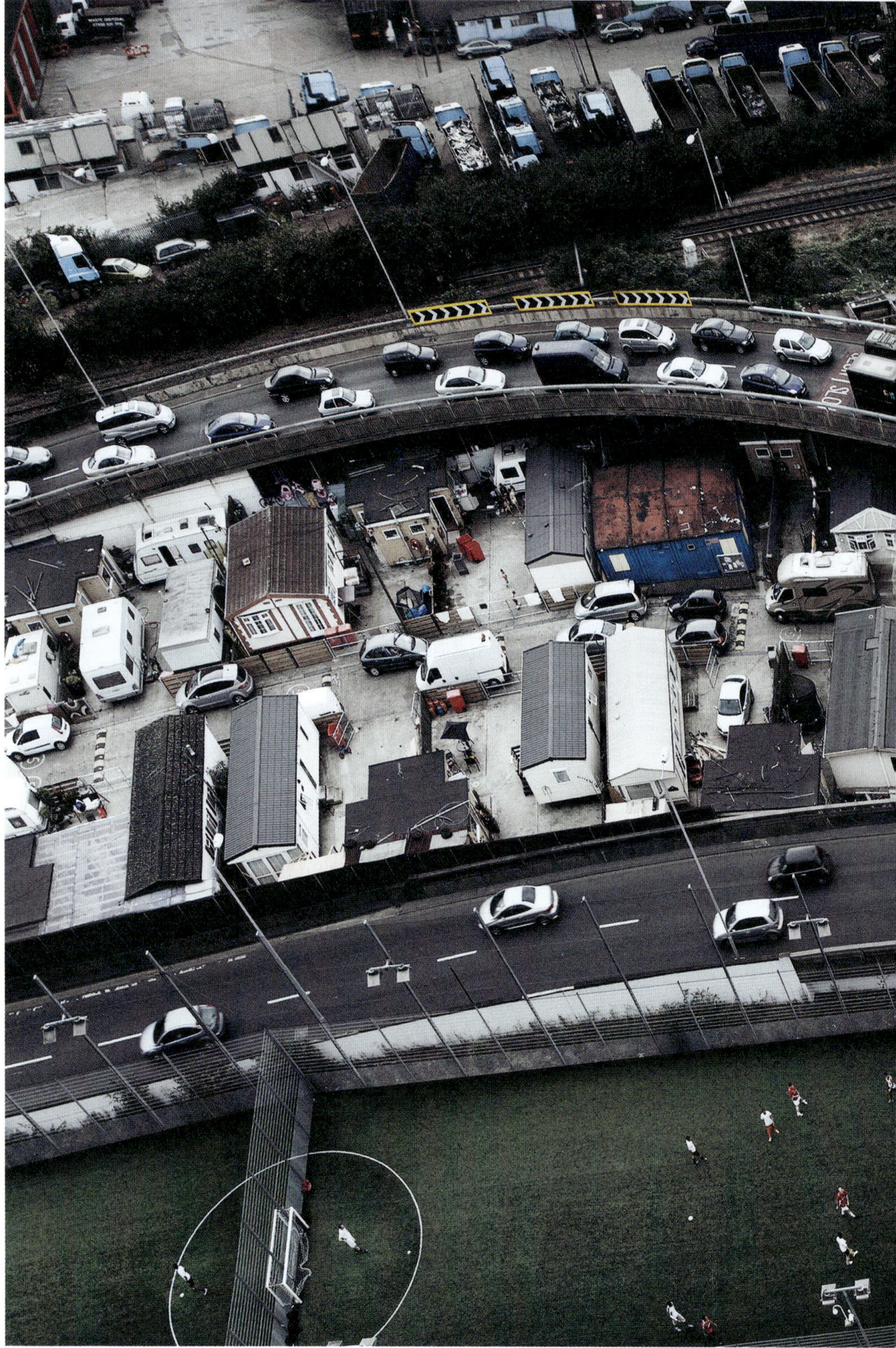

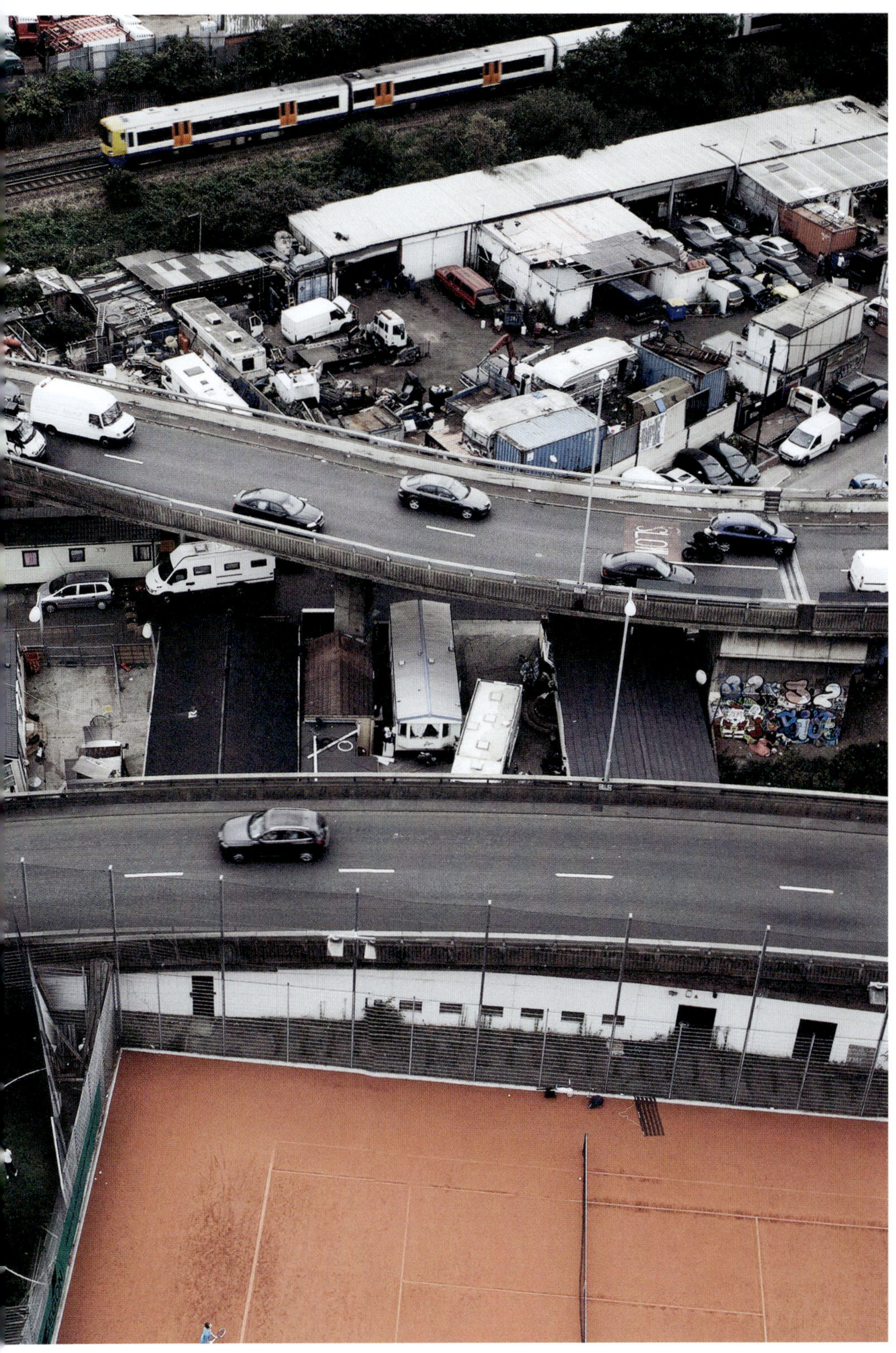

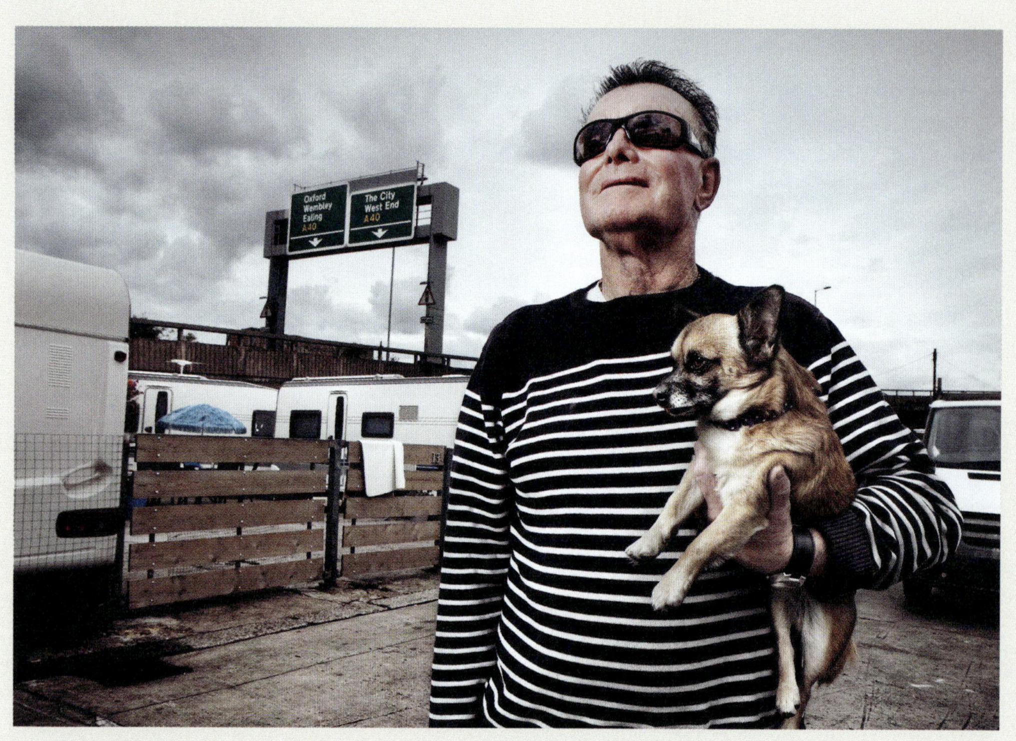

Oxford
Wembley
Ealing
A40
The City
West End
A40

MARTI'S STORY

Marti was one of the very first Travellers to live on the site and moved there when it wasn't an official Traveller site over 40 years ago. He was a lovely guy and this is his story. Sadly, he passed away just a few years after I had finished the project.

I came to this part of London to see my father, he was camping out under the flyover, and I haven't left. That was 40-odd years ago.

We stayed under the flyover for two-and-a-half years and were quite happy, no one was bothering us. They were just finishing off the flyover and they were knocking down lots of the old houses, the ones that look like Coronation Street. Then the council gave everybody a letter telling us to move off because we weren't there legally. So I went to see a lawyer to get the eviction stopped. Then a couple of months later I was in my caravan and three men from the council came and said they wanted to make us a site for 20 families.

Two years later the site was built and I thought it was a very good thing. They had to put the news in the local papers and when they did the local people were all up in arms. They didn't want us there but it was the council's duty to help us. The government had said they had to find sites for us, as it was no longer acceptable to force us off.

We knew it was going to be a fantastic thing because we would get an education for our families and for my grandchildren. It was something we could never get when we were travelling about, getting one week here and one week there. Then a terrible thing happened: the night before we were due to move in, the local people broke up the place with sledgehammers. You can't imagine what it feels like to be a Traveller when they come and smash up your home. We weren't bothering anybody. We just wanted a home so we could get an education for the kids and our families. The council put guards on the site and the workmen came and rebuilt it all which took another eight months. We moved in and we were so happy to be there.

Eight years later we found out that they were going to take the site off us and not provide any other site. The local people signed a petition to get rid of us from the area and the council said, 'Your time is up and you have so many weeks to move off'. I went to see a lawyer and told them what was going on and we took the council to court. We found a barrister to take the case on, he said he would do it for free as it would be a good experience for him. It went on for years, but in the end the court said that this site was not fit for human habitation and there shouldn't be anybody living under the flyover. But the judge said the site was to stay where it was and the council must look for more ground if they want us to move. We had won the case!

The locals did not accept it so we were taken to court again and they got all the signatures again. We only went to the magistrates' court this time and it was chucked out the same day. So we are still here!

Travelling people like to get into sites and settle down because the kids can go to secondary school and college. There are an awful lot of travellers still going about that have no home at all and all they want to do is settle down somewhere. They keep being made to move on to someone else's patch and are always unwelcome. Today, most travellers only move if they want to go to the races or the fair. The days of travelling around all the time finished years ago. The generation that are coming up don't want to travel, so in another 50 or 60 years the travelling life will be gone forever. Some travelling people are getting married to Gorgers – that's what we call people who are not travellers.

When I came here in the 1960s and I looked for a place to stay, there were signs in the windows: 'No Irish, No Blacks and No Dogs!' If you walked into a pub 25 years ago with several travellers together they would say 'We don't want Gypsies in here and the lot of you are barred'. Discrimination is still here, it's hard to book a party for a wedding if they know you're a Gypsy for example, but it's got much, much better.

Back at the start, we were offered the land because it was of no use for anything else and was worth nothing. Now the planning rules have changed and you can build here and the land has become worth a lot. I reckon in another three or four years they're going to come and say, 'Look, we are going to close the site down and we cannot provide anything else unless you go into bricks and mortar'. We don't want to go into bricks and mortar, as you lose all your identity. We would all get split up and housed separately. You could end up with your son living 10 miles away and that would be the end of our traveller culture. We said no to being split up.

If you go back to the 60s when lots of immigrants came to England, they wanted to all live together and they did. So this goes back to all kinds of cultures, not just ours. We want to be together. People stay together to keep their culture and identity; we feel safer this way, we look out for each other.

We have been told about plans to redevelop the area where we live, the stables, the mechanics' garages and the other side of the railway line. I think it's ridiculous, they are not thinking about local people. The regeneration should be for people who have lived here for 100s of years but it's not, it's for new people. The leisure centre will get more tennis courts and there will be expensive flats looking down at us. It's all for the rich folk, it's not for us or people like us! They just want to break us up and destroy our culture.

A traveller doesn't really care where they go, as long as there are six or seven families together. It's our culture, it's our way. Until they give the travellers the rights to build their own sites these problems will not go away. We don't want to lose who we are. If you settle down in a house you might not see another traveller for two or three years. We are part of this country and we have a right to keep our culture just like all the others.

Marti Ward
London, 2014

THANKS

I want to say a massive thank you to Pat, who has become a good friend. Without him, I would not have been able to make this book. Like me, he realised the importance of showing the Travellers as they really are, not as they are portrayed on sensationalised television programmes.

Thanks to Winnie O'Donnell and all the family. All The Westway Travellers Community for putting up with me nosing around, day after day. Phil Regan, especially for the V&A exhibition. Sarah Tuvey at The Westway Stables. Sarah Cooper, Head Teacher at Oxford Gardens School. The Arts University Bournemouth and the staff who gave me so much support. Professor Stuart Bartholomew CBE, Professor Emma Hunt, Valerie Lodge and Paul Allen.

Paul Wenham-Clarke
London, 2019

Urban Gypsies

First edition

Copyright © Hoxton Mini Press 2019. All rights reserved.

All photographs © Paul Wenham-Clarke
Introduction text by Rachel Segal Hamilton
Afterword text by Marti Ward
Design and sequence by Friederike Huber

A CIP catalogue record for this book is available from the British Library

ISBN 978-1-910566-49-7

First published in the United Kingdom in 2019 by Hoxton Mini Press

No part of this publication may be reproduced, stored in a retrieval system,
or transmitted in any form or by any means, electronic, mechanical,
photocopying, recording or otherwise, without the prior written
permissionof the copyright owner.

Repro by Touch Digital. Production, design and editorial support from
Anna De Pascale, Daniele Roa and Faith McAllister at Hoxton Mini Press.

Printed and bound by Livonia, Latvia

To order books, collector's editions and signed prints please go to:
www.hoxtonminipress.com

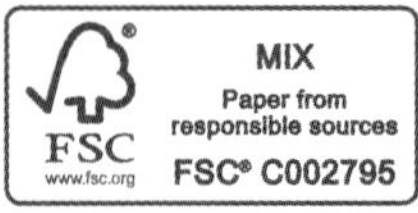